# PUPPET OR PUPPETEER: CHOOSE THE LIFE YOU WANT TO LIVE

## *A COMPANION GUIDEBOOK*

NELL M. RODGERS, DC, MN, RN

Copyright © 2006 by Dr. Nell M. Rodgers

All rights reserved. No part of this work may be reproduced or transmitted in any form by any means, electronic or mechanical, including photocopying and recording, or by any information storage or retrieval system, except as may be expressly permitted by the 1976 Copyright Act or in writing by the publisher.

Awesome Press, Inc.
P. O. Box 1071
Decatur, GA  30031-1071

Rodgers, Dr. Nell M.
   Puppet or Puppeteer: Choose the Life You Want to Live: A Companion Workbook

Layout: J. L. Saloff
Fonts: New Century Schoolbook; Capitals
Cover Design: Mary Fisher Design

10 Digit ISBN: 0-9745240-2-6
13 Digit ISBN: 978-0-9745240-2-3

      Library of Congress Control Number: 2006909995

*First Edition*

*Printed in the United State of America on acid free paper.*

# DEDICATION

*This book is Lovingly Dedicated to:*

*Dr. Theresa Pigott*
*Dr. Gale Keppel*
*and*
*Ms. Jamie Saloff*

*"To know what you prefer instead of humbly saying Amen to what the world tells you you ought to prefer, is to have kept your soul alive."*

Robert Louis Stevenson
1850-1894

# TABLE OF CONTENTS

**INTRODUCTION** .................................................................1

**PART I: LET'S GET PERSONAL!** ...........................................5

    You Are Blessed .................................................................11
    You Are Praiseworthy ........................................................12
    Exploiting Your Abilities Decreases Doubt ......................12
    Winning Comes From Within ...........................................13
    Mistakes Are Opportunities to Learn and Exist Only in the
        Eye of the Beholder ...................................................13
    Victimization Is Impossible Without Permission .............14
    Victims Never Have Fullness of Life ................................15
    Sharing Feelings Is a Way of Sharing Yourself and Being Authentic ...........16
    Anxiety "Attacks" Are Nonexistent and Stem ..................18
    From Unconscious Beliefs .................................................18
    The Only Approval You Need Is From Yourself .............19
    All Worry Is Useless ..........................................................20
    Positive Thinking Engenders Positive Living ..................21
    Fear Is Living in the Future ..............................................23
    Guilt Is Living in the Past .................................................24
    Guilt Is Searching for Punishment ...................................26
    Now Is All You Have ........................................................27
    Anger Stems From Helplessness .......................................28
    Resentment Requires Commitment ..................................29
    Resentment Punishes the Person Holding the Resentment ......................35
    Emotions Are the Result of Thoughts and Beliefs ..........35
    You Are in Charge of What You Feel (Your Emotions) ......................36
    Anger and Resentment Keep You Stuck in Victimization .........38
    You Are Perfect Just the Way You Are ............................40
    Results Come From Actions Related to Desires ..............41
    Self-Disclosure Is Growth .................................................42
    Shame Comes From Within ..............................................43
    Turn Your Negative Statements Into Positive Statements ........48
    Your Thoughts and Behaviors Determine Your Skills and
        Excellence ..................................................................50
    Martyrdom Is Certain Doom ............................................54
    Rewarding Yourself Is Motivating ....................................58

Feelings Are Your Barometer ................................................. 58
Power Originates From Within ................................................ 60
Living With Purpose Creates Fullness of Life ................................. 64
Expressing Gratitude Is Healing .............................................. 67
Needing Permission Sets up a Child/Parent Relationship Which
   Disallows Evolved Behavior ................................................ 69
Love of Self Comes From the Self ............................................. 70
Create a Private Magic Zone in Your Mind ..................................... 70
Play Brings Magic, Healing and Joy to Life ................................... 71
Stretching Your Limits Is a Way to Grow and Transform ........................ 72
Routine Assessment and Monitoring Lets You Know Where
   You Are Now and Where You Are Headed ..................................... 75
Specific Circumstances Call for Explicit Decisions ........................... 78
Resolute Principles and Values Are Your Governing Force ...................... 79
Your Life Is Declaration of Your Beliefs ..................................... 80
An Integrity Inventory Will Reflect Your Self-Worth .......................... 81
Reviewing Where You Are Can Open New Doors ................................... 83
Expanded Thinking Decreases Angst ............................................ 86
Giving Yourself Permission Is Vital To a Full and Fulfilling Life ............ 86
Knowing Where You Are Optimizes Potential for Change ......................... 88
Shifting From Negative to Positive Self-Talk Is Empowering ................... 89
Disengaging From the Past Facilitates Increased Knowledge of,
   and Engagement With the Present .......................................... 92
Cliche´ - Beliefs Can Be Misleading and Self-Defeating ....................... 93
What You See May Be What You Want to Believe ................................. 95
Gratitude Cultivates Contentment, Giving Engenders Self-Love ................. 96
Your Behavior Reflects Your Self-Judgment .................................... 97
Following Through on Commitments Is the Path to Obtaining
   Goals .................................................................... 98
Feeding Your Spirit Is Its Own Reward ........................................ 99
Giving Permission Means Something Is Authorized and
   Sanctioned ............................................................... 101
Pulling Your Own Strings Requires Clarity and Personal Focus ................. 103

# APPENDIX: RESOURCES, INFORMATION AND PRACTITIONERS ...... 115

# ABOUT THE AUTHOR ........................................... 129

# Acknowledgments

I offer genuine appreciation and sincere gratitude to my: friends, colleagues, associates, family, and especially, to those readers who advocated the creation of this workbook.

The list is much too long to include everyone individually by name. However, I want each of you to know that I am deeply grateful for your continuing, unwavering and loving support. Your feedback and encouragement has been important and meaningful in the fullest sense.

Thank you.

I wish for each of you an empowered and rich life.

# INTRODUCTION

Some people lead an empowered life; one in which they attain goals and create joy . Others have a ho-hum life. Still others are always striving, or feel their passion is thwarted. In writing *Puppet or Puppeteer: Choose the Life You Want to Live*, my intent was to assist people in transforming themselves; to help them learn how to be in charge of their own situations and lives; to provide information which can be used in moments of angst as well as on a daily basis. Many readers have expressed appreciation for the depth and breadth of information given there. At the same time, reader responses indicate that people wanted more.

Feedback has led to the creation of a personal, accessory work book. Although this guidebook has been written based on many of the principles presented in *Puppet or Puppeteer*, it also stands alone. You may use the book without association to *Puppet or Puppeteer* or in conjunction with that book. Either way, you will receive the benefits of the program. The necessary part is that you begin. By routinely scheduling yourself to do the exercises, you will be moving toward being all that you can be, letting go of struggle and more easily

*"In the eyes of God <u>everyone</u> is coded to be a star."*
  Marianne Williamson

obtaining your goals. You can be rid of a ho-hum, yearning existence. You can pull your own strings; be your own puppeteer. You can live the life you choose and choose the life you live.

Some of your beliefs are in opposition to your desires and dreams. In fact, you hold certain hidden beliefs which are the undercurrent of all that you do. They exist whether or not you are aware of them; whether or not you want them to be a part of who you are. The information in this guidebook is designed to assist you in learning about your own habits, personal behavior patterns, and the explicit beliefs which currently direct your life. There are times when your hidden beliefs actually block your progress and squelch your dreams. This workbook offers ways to change that. You have the opportunity to literally formulate new beliefs and to utilize beliefs which actually further your progress and boost your energy. Specific exercises for your personal belief modification, along with methods and practices for distinct change are presented.

By design, there is a duality in the presentation. First, the header statements are concepts which stand alone. They are applicable to your personal development as you look at ways of living a full and fulfilling life. Each can also be used as an affirmation, quote for the day, posting as a conspicuous reminder, or similar uses. When using the book this way, you may simply go to the table of contents to view the header statements. You may also look for information about a particular subject in *Puppet or Puppeteer*. The contents under each header statement may also help you further understand the concept contained within the statement.

A more comprehensive and valuable way to use the book is to take time to do all the exercises listed under the various headings. You will bring the concepts alive in a totally different way. The exercises are designed to improve, modify or change how you look at yourself and your own personal situation(s). By completing them, you will begin to see the development of new beliefs which compliment your desired life changes and promote your dreams. Since every person is unique, shifts and personal growth will be specific to you. Your rate of personal growth as well as your privacy will be controlled by you.

Many of the exercises are designed so that they may be used over and over. For example, a question related to being in charge of what you feel is: "What three things can you do today to counteract each of your most negative emotions?" The answers to this question will probably be different now then they will be in a six months or a year from now. If you are currently working on feelings of timidity, you may be working on feelings of anger and resentment next year. In other words, as you change, the information needed to complete the exercises will also change. This means that you can continue to use this workbook for years to come. Quite an investment, eh?

If the amount of work presented or depth of answers requested feels intimidating or overwhelming, please look at the questions independently. Implement the exercises at a comfortable speed for you and your own process. There is no "rush-to-completion" requirement. This work is for you. The only urgency is that you persistently chip away at that which is unwanted in your life. That is because the work that you do here is done as basic preparation for living the life you desire. Remember, life is a process. Personal growth is a continuous undertaking.

# A Companion Guidebook

Begin your work with practical amounts of activity and keep it manageable. This workbook is not one in which you read, "fill in the blanks" until the pages are full and then set it aside. It is a work that you will come back to again and again as you desire more and more change. Change requires energy and focus. Both the content and exercises are geared toward an ongoing process of introspection and implementation. By going to these pages repeatedly and consistently, you will develop the habit of self-observation. When you have done so, change will come much more quickly based on decisions that use your own personal feedback.

The workbook is divided into two parts. First there are a series of statements of truth with their accompanying exercises. Secondly, there are descriptions of the body's energy centers along with related, complementary focusing/relaxing practices. The first part of the guidebook is designed to help you look at where you are now and where you want to go; to help you with the design of who you wish to be in terms of tapping into your authentic self. This is done through looking at your feelings and actions in the present. Are you judgmental of yourself? Do you overextend to others? Are there any tendencies toward being a victim or martyr? Does guilt play a part in your life? These are tough topics and there are some tough questions, but the work does not have to be difficult. Generally, the most difficult part will be mustering the discipline to stay on tract. The program does require honesty and integrity. If you are not honest with yourself, that is probably how you live your entire life. For this work, you will go absolutely nowhere unless you are honest in your responses. Becoming your own puppeteer requires that you have integrity.

There probably will be moments when you wonder if anything is happening; if any change is occurring. These are the times in which you must compel yourself to stay with the work. Old habits sometimes die hard and it often seems easier just to stick with the same ole behaviors. The fact that you raise the question as to whether change is occurring, is, in itself the answer. The ego does not want you to change. It wants you to remain the same and therefore will play such games in its attempt to halt you. When you are in charge and feeling your wisdom and inner power, what happens to the ego? You got it! The ego begins to disappear. The good news is that in its place is a clarity of purpose and sense of confidence. Keep the work going on schedule, even if your intention is to do one page each month. Every step you take, puts you closer to pulling your own strings.

In the second part of the book, the energy centers of the body are addressed. More elaborate detail is given about each center in *Puppet or Puppeteer*. However, I have included in the guidebook sufficient information to give you an overview of each center. There is data which will assist you in knowing which center you may want to work with at any given time. For example, if you are grieving, the center which controls the lungs and the emotion of grieving would probably bring comfort and additional clarity. Based on the same data you may also come to understand the necessity for keeping each of these centers "clear" and fluid.

A meditation/relaxation exercise for each center is given along with the basic information about that center,. They are designed so that you may read them into a tape recorder and listen to your own words as you go through the experience(s). I encourage you to record some of the programs now so that when the moment comes to use them, you will be ready. In a critical moment, you can then access them freely. You are also encouraged to take the information provided and create your own programs of relaxation. Design them to meet to your personal needs.

# Puppet or Puppeteer / Dr. Nell Rodgers

Keep all these materials as your own. This will provide privacy and confidence. If you decide to share them, be certain that you are making a conscience choice to do so. Then, share them only with those whom you can totally trust.

The Appendix provides information about where to go for help. I have been very selective and included only those professionals or organizations whose work dovetails with this guidebook. They will be of value in keeping you headed in a singular direction. Tapping into these resources can help if and when you feel torn about what action to take, feel stuck, do not know what to do, or feel pulled in more than one direction.

The reference Section will be invaluable for adding to your understanding of the concepts I have presented. Please supplement your work with extensive reading. The work in this guidebook is comprehensive but certainly not all encompassing. Continue to explore and venture outside the common way. Go beyond ordinary behaviors and responses. New discoveries can come at any time and with increasing frequency. But you must be open, ready and willing.

It is my sincere desire that this workbook will provide the guidance you need as you step onto a path which welcomes new growth opportunities. It is my dream for you that you will accept the challenge to pull your own strings; to be your own puppeteer; to create the life you really want to live.

# Part I: Let's Get Personal!

This workbook will assist you in actively redesigning your life. By following these guidelines you begin to create the life you want. It will take some work. However, by closely examining your feelings, behaviors, habits and beliefs you can do it. You are given an opportunity to analyze your life and formulate specific new directions for yourself. With focus and action you can make decisions and changes which reflect your own individual beliefs, actions and desires. These questions and statements, your consistency in answering with integrity, and the manner in which you utilize the information can be invaluable in your personal growth. In short, you can take charge and direct your own life.

By design, this book is best when used in conjunction with *Puppet or Puppeteer: Choose the Life You Want to Live*. However, this is not expedient. You can still benefit from any and all the exercises presented. Some people may want to work with a group in order to have moral support. This is fine. Just remember the importance of making it *your* work. Keep in front of you at all times, the fact that your goal is to be become your own puppeteer. Let the group be a support

*Eliminate something superfluous from your life. Break a habit. Do something that makes you feel insecure.*

Piero Ferrucci

*"Every day you may make progress. Every step may be fruitful. Yet there will stretch out before you an ever-lengthening, ever-ascending, ever-improving path. You know you will never get to the end of the journey. But this, so far from discouraging, only adds to the joy and glory of the climb."*

Sir Winston Churchill,
(1874-1965)

and not a determining factor in your actions and decisions. Choosing how to use the book is yet another way in which you can flex your creative skills.

You are asked to respond to numerous questions throughout the book. This is purposeful. When we ask questions of ourselves, the brain/mind engages in a comprehensive, all encompassing quest for the perfect answer. Your conscious and subconscious mind will automatically search through your entire brain, *all* cellular systems, and any related external information in order to give you the perfect answer. This is much like a relentless, highly motivated research scientist who might search through a complete library to come up with a particular answer. Personal computers, when asked to do so, can search the entire hard drive for a specific file. Your brain/mind automatically does the same thing when you ask for personal information. All aspects of you, the "human computer," will be searched completely. The answer to your question will be given. This means that the numbers and types of questions you ask are extremely significant. If you ask why "rotten things" always happen to you, your brain will give you the reasons why "rotten things" happen to you. If you ask for the most appropriate next step, you will be given that information. Whatever you focus on, the brain/mind (which includes the subconscious) must also focus on. It is exquisitely important to understand this concept.

By asking specific questions, you get specific, descriptive information and the types of answers you seek. Asking negative questions yields negative responses. Asking questions which promote your desires and goals yields information which supports what you want. When you regularly ask positive questions such as, "How can I more quickly and legally increase my cash flow?" you will be given information about that. When we only make statements, we are not using the brain/mind's ability to assist us in getting the information we need to move forward. In addition, statements tend to become factual. For example, "With my luck, I'll probably loose out," is a statement which sets you up for repetitious loss or "bad luck." Soon, you begin to think of yourself as a loser or as incapable of bringing "good luck" into your life. Next, you act as if you are a loser and literally begin to fail in some area or aspect of your life. It is to your advantage when you make statements about yourself or your intentions, to be sure they are stated in a positive way.

Repeatedly asking questions of yourself establishes a habit for the brain. It is much like building a muscle. Practice is required. The more you practice, the more quickly and automatically the answers will come. In time, you begin to get information with little, if any, effort. It becomes obvious that for the best results, you must ask questions which take you in the direction of your desires rather than questions which confirm your worst or negative concerns and fears. Get into the habit of creating questions which represent the outcome that you want. Suppose you are struggling with a situation or issue you neither understand nor want in your life. You want to know how to remedy or change the situation. Often, in such moments, we ask, "Why is this happening to me?" A more rewarding and powerful question to ask is, "What can I do right now that will change what is happening to me?" After all, an action is probably the answer you actually want. Who cares "why" this is happening? The issue is, how can you stop it?

By asking your subconscious the same questions over and over again, you can actually program yourself to remain in a rut of unwanted behavior. The question, "What is wrong with me?" literally yields a list of symptoms or negative attributes or behaviors. The question, "Why can't I do anything right," will cause your brain/mind to give you a list of reasons which verify that you cannot do things "right." The brain is, by design, obligated to give answers to your questions. As the saying goes, "Garbage in, garbage out." Negative, old, and repetitious questions keep you tied to the behaviors you may be attempting to avoid.

When you ask streamlined, specific questions which seek positive, goal-related answers, you are on your way to becoming your own puppeteer. A bit more response time or repetition of certain questions may be required because, in most of us, there is lack of habitual optimistic reference for the subconscious. We seem to have that programmed *out* of us as we grow up. Most people are well versed and extensively trained in disparaging or unfavorable inner dialog, often forgetting self-praise and positive thinking. How often have you executed a task quite well, even were complimented? Yet, you focused on the one slip-of-the-tongue or some equally innocuous related behavior. I am almost embarrassed to recall how many times I have created a nice project from wood only to apologize for its lack of perfection when others commented on its beauty. This is how we maintain our minimized self; the way we keep our inner wisdom and beauty subdued.

The subconscious has perfect answers for both positive and negative questions; both status quo maintenance and growth-producing inquiries. Use the wisdom and vast knowledge of the subconscious to help you achieve what you want. I cannot overemphasize that constructive self-healing responses and growth-producing ideas will present themselves when appropriate questions are asked with clarity, frequency and focused intention. Here are examples of questions to avoid and questions to ask.

1. "Why can't I get ahead in life?" becomes: "How can I create a job situation that will provide a minimum of "X" dollars per week while bringing excitement into my life?" "How can I find work that is both satisfying and financially rewarding?"

2. "How come I am stuck with being fat?" becomes: "What can I do today to bring myself closer to my goal of eliminating "X" pounds of excess weight?" "What purpose is my weight serving?" "Is there a better or more healthy way to get those needs met?"

3. "Why does "X" always happen to me?" becomes: "What behavior can I change to eliminate "X" from my life?" "What can I do to prevent "X" from happening to me?" "Is there something valuable or positive that I can focus on when "X" happens to me?"

In each of these examples the first question is focusing on unwanted and negative aspects of yourself or your goal. In fact, they actually affirm the unwanted. The second question is precise, specific and calls on the brain and subconscious to supply information which supports that which is desired; actions to be taken which bring you toward your preferences. Once again, for good measure, choice is always available and the subconscious will always give the answers you seek.

# Puppet or Puppeteer / Dr. Nell Rodgers

Does it not make sense to phrase questions which push your subconscious to assist you in getting what you want?

How many times have you stood in a long line and said something like, "I always choose the slowest line." In that moment, you are affirming that this is and will be your pattern. The questions you ask yourself and the affirmations you proclaim can be the difference between resignation and responsible personal growth. It can actually be the difference between being miserable and feeling joyful. In this situation, you could just as easily ask, "How can I get out of this store more quickly?" while at the same time scanning with your eyes and ears for new or different opportunities. For example, at times, I ask people if I might go ahead of them since I only have one or two items. People usually are nice enough to permit you to bend the rules a little. Of course, instead of being angry, I am smiling and congenial as I ask. And, I do have wrinkled skin and white hair! Never-the-less, you can have equal success if you focus on what you want instead of asking the negative questions or validating an unwanted situation or action as truth by stating it.

All the questions in this book are phrased to give answers which, when implemented, can more rapidly move you toward your goals or desires. You may use this workbook as you would use a text workbook in a classroom. Even though you are not reaching for a high academic grade, you are establishing patterns that will make you your own puppeteer. The exercises are designed to help you practice and get comfortable with the kinds of questions to ask. At the same time, the responses will guide you steadily toward being who and what you want to be.

Some parts of the first section are designed to elicit information which will help you become more aware of how you function, what your deeper emotions are and which beliefs are driving you in unwanted directions. Respond, even though you may feel uncomfortable. Persistence in responding to these questions and other issues will put you on course. You will be rewarded by knowing and experiencing that you and no one else is in the driver's seat for your life. This work is an investment in yourself and your future. Since it is for you, it need only be seen by you. So, take time to respond with integrity and authenticity. That will bring the best results.

Some of the questions ask for information which you might feel is inaccessible. Some, you may wish to avoid because they feel painful or because you fear what you may "awaken" from other times in your life. Take the risk. Ask the questions anyway. Keep asking until the answers come. Be willing to hear the answers. Remain open to your feelings. Be willing to take action. Remember that appropriate questions are a gateway to change. You will, of course, have other questions and data which need responses as you proceed. The intention here is to give examples of how you can structure your personal growth and your "change-your-life" activities with the greatest benefit. You may use the information as it is or as a guide for creating your own processes.

Use Section II of *Puppet or Puppeteer: Choose the Life You Want to Live* to assist you as you look at specific exercises. Using the readings found there can be useful in implementing almost any of the exercises in this workbook. For instance, when considering setting up a quiet space, refer to the readings, "On Meditation," "On Commitment," "On Decisions" or other readings which you feel might be related or helpful. Another example: when completing the exercises presented under "Victimization Is Impossible Without Permission" in this guidebook, read "On Victim" in

# A Companion Guidebook

*Puppet or Puppeteer: Choose the Life You Want to Live.* You will then have background information to help you sort out some of the data or feelings you experience as you go through the assignment. Part two of this guidebook can also be easily integrated with your work in part One.

The introspective activities in this guidebook may be used whenever you desire, and in any order you prefer. Many promote change quickly. Some will require a bit longer before you experience change. Some will need to be repeated from time to time. Still others are designed to allow you to use them repeatedly but in relation to different situations or periods in your life. Many readers will advance through the exercises sequentially. Choose those which feel the most appropriate, the most important time-wise, or ask for inner guidance. One exercise may take several days or you may complete several exercises in a short period of time. Personal growth is an ongoing process. Follow your intuitive guide.

Our minds are bursting with information upon awakening. Research has shown that writing immediately upon getting out of bed is exceptionally productive. Our minds are fresh and uncluttered. We are more creative because the stress and requirements of the day are not yet upon us. Dreams have stirred our subconscious, often yielding rich sources of "inside information" for exploration, release and potential belief changes. In fact, Julia Cameron in her book, *The Artist's Way* recommends hand writing a minimum of three pages the very first thing each morning. I suggest that you consider keeping this guidebook near your bed. Use it as soon as you get up. You may be amazed at the difference in how the questions and exercises are answered or experienced as a result of tapping into your mind while it is unencumbered.

I suggest that you have a separate notebook for additional entries related to your experiences. First, you may feel you want to do more than the allotted space in the book permits. Following your intuition and your hunches about this is quite valuable. Your subconscious knows where to take you. Secondly, handwriting answers is more powerful than typing responses into a computer or typewriter. Writing gives your inner voice a way of presenting itself. When writing, your feelings are given expression that does not come when typing, or even talking. Your pen becomes an extension of you. Amazing things can happen. Interesting information will surface. New insights can be gained. You may go in a direction that you had not envisioned.

Fill this guidebook with notes, answers, self-information, intrapersonal discussions and all sorts of self-growth messages and reminders. I suggest that you keep your notes in a private place so that you feel safe to express anything and everything which comes through.

I will be with you in spirit. Let's get started!

# A Companion Guidebook

## YOU ARE BLESSED
*(See: On Gratitude)*

- List a minimum of 20 times in your life that something *wonderful* or positive happened without your overt assistance or provocation.

_____    _____
_____    _____
_____    _____
_____    _____
_____    _____
_____    _____
_____    _____
_____    _____
_____    _____
_____    _____

- Read this list a minimum of ten times per month for three months. Record each reading on the chart below along with why you are thankful on that day. This will remind you and your unconscious of the wonder of life.

_____  _____  _____
_____  _____  _____
_____  _____  _____
_____  _____  _____
_____  _____  _____
_____  _____  _____

# Puppet or Puppeteer / Dr. Nell Rodgers

## You Are Praiseworthy
*(See: On Loving Yourself)*

- List a minimum of ten outstanding abilities you now have.

_____    _____
_____    _____
_____    _____
_____    _____
_____    _____


## Exploiting Your Abilities Decreases Doubt
*(See: On Claiming Your Power)*

- What can you do to assure that you begin each day with an awareness and acknowledgement of at least two of your abilities?

_____
_____
_____
_____

- On what date are you willing to commit to doing this?

_____    _____
_____    _____
_____    _____

## WINNING COMES FROM WITHIN
*(See: On Claiming Your Power, On Releasing)*

- List the times/situations that bother you most in which you thought yourself to be a loser.

_____    _____
_____    _____
_____    _____
_____    _____

- What could you have done in each situation that would have made you feel like a winner deep inside yourself?

_____
_____
_____
_____
_____
_____

## MISTAKES ARE OPPORTUNITIES TO LEARN AND EXIST ONLY IN THE EYE OF THE BEHOLDER

- List five mistakes you think you made this month and the emotional reaction you had to each.

_____
_____
_____
_____

## Puppet or Puppeteer / Dr. Nell Rodgers

- How could you have responsibly experienced and expressed the feeling related to each incident?

_____
_____
_____
_____
_____

- What steps will you now take to forgive yourself for each perceived faux pas and move on?

_____
_____
_____
_____
_____

## Victimization Is Impossible Without Permission
*(See: On Victim)*

- List ten times you think you have been a victim.

_____   _____
_____   _____
_____   _____
_____   _____
_____   _____

# A COMPANION GUIDEBOOK

- What are five ways you can change your response to persons who may attempt to victimize you while at the same time claiming your inner power?

_____

_____

_____

_____

_____

_____

## VICTIMS NEVER HAVE FULLNESS OF LIFE
*(See: On Claiming Your Power)*

- What new affirmation will you use and what new belief will you reprogram that will assist you as you give up your victimization? When?

## Puppet or Puppeteer / Dr. Nell Rodgers

- Program These Beliefs to Increase Your Personal Well-Being:

    - I let go of being a victim and all victim identity.

        Date completed: _____

    - I am free to take control of my life and calmly stand in my personal authentic power.

        Date completed: _____

    - I am responsible for my responses to all situations.

        Date completed: _____

    - It is OK to live my life in freedom and to respond to my own desires.

        Date completed: _____

    - It is OK to say, "Stop doing this to me."

        Date completed: _____

    - I forgive all who may have "victimized" me.

        Date completed: _____

    - I am ready, willing and able to access, experience and appropriately express my innermost feelings.

        Date completed: _____

## SHARING FEELINGS IS A WAY OF SHARING YOURSELF AND BEING AUTHENTIC
*(See: On Self-Disclosure, On Risk-Taking)*

- List all the feelings you remember experiencing today (positive & negative).

    _____        _____
    _____        _____
    _____        _____
    _____        _____

*(continues...)*

# A Companion Guidebook

_____          _____
_____          _____
_____          _____
_____          _____
_____          _____

- Who are three people you trust to share your innermost feelings? Do they trust you?

_____          _____
_____          _____
_____          _____
_____          _____

- What are three ways you can go about sharing a minimum of three previously hidden feelings within the next five days?

_____
_____
_____
_____
_____
_____
_____
_____
_____
_____

## Anxiety "Attacks" Are Nonexistent and Stem From Unconscious Beliefs

*(See: On Fear, On Claiming Your Power, On Feeling Emotions)*

- List a minimum of ten situations or experiences you believe cause you to feel anxious.

- What are 24 personal changes you can make to decrease or eliminate anxiety?

# A Companion Guidebook

- What new belief can you program to alleviate your anxiety in each situation? (The new beliefs may be the same or overlap.) When?

_____     _____
_____     _____
_____     _____
_____     _____
_____     _____
_____     _____
_____     _____
_____     _____
_____     _____
_____     _____
_____     _____

## THE ONLY APPROVAL YOU NEED IS FROM YOURSELF
*(See: On Internal vs. External Control)*

- List the negative things you most often believe others think about you; even the small things.

_____   _____   _____
_____   _____   _____
_____   _____   _____
_____   _____   _____

## Puppet or Puppeteer / Dr. Nell Rodgers

- List two positive statements you will make about yourself that counteract or offset each thing on this list?

_____    _____
_____    _____
_____    _____
_____    _____
_____    _____
_____    _____
_____    _____

## All Worry Is Useless
*(See: On Getting Going, On Decisions, On Problem Solving)*

- List the worries that waste your time and energy (now and in the past).

_____    _____
_____    _____
_____    _____
_____    _____
_____    _____

- What are two constructive actions you can take in relation to *each* of the worries listed?

_____    _____
_____    _____
_____    _____

*(continues...)*

### A Companion Guidebook

_____   _____
_____   _____
_____   _____
_____   _____
_____   _____
_____   _____
_____   _____
_____   _____
_____   _____

- On what date will you take action in relation to *each* worry?

_____   _____   _____
_____   _____   _____
_____   _____   _____
_____   _____   _____

- Write down all the times your worries turned out to be truths. *(Hint: There are none.)*

## Positive Thinking Engenders Positive Living
*(See: Section I, Chapter 2)*

- What concrete actions can I take to train myself to look for something positive in all my experiences?

_____
_____

*(continues. . .)*

## Puppet or Puppeteer / Dr. Nell Rodgers

_____
_____
_____
_____
_____
_____
_____
_____

- What are five benefits I will gain when I look for the positive aspects of my experiences?

_____
_____
_____
_____
_____

- What behaviors can I use to reprogram my thinking and behavior so that I consistently acknowledge the positive elements of my life?

_____
_____
_____
_____
_____
_____
_____
_____

## Fear Is Living in the Future

- List five activities or problems that you feel fearful about.

_____
_____
_____
_____
_____

- What is the thing you fear most about each of these five experiences?

_____
_____
_____
_____
_____

- What action(s) can you take to reduce or eliminate the fear in each? Schedule at least four actions to be taken within the next two weeks.

| Action: | Date Scheduled: |
| --- | --- |
| _____ | _____ |
| _____ | _____ |
| _____ | _____ |
| _____ | _____ |
| _____ | _____ |
| _____ | _____ |

## Puppet or Puppeteer / Dr. Nell Rodgers

## Guilt Is Living in the Past
*(See: On Guilt, On Forgiveness, On Now, On Responsibility)*

- List ten behaviors, thoughts or situations about which you feel or have felt guilty.

_____
_____
_____
_____
_____
_____
_____
_____
_____
_____

- List three people, situations or acts about which you now have guilt.

_____  _____
_____  _____

- Make a decision to eliminate the guilt. On what date(s) will you settle differences or apologize in a manner that ends your guilt in relation to each person, situation or act? Include forgiveness of yourself. What will you do in each instance? Schedule the dates on your calendar.

| Action: | Date Scheduled: |
|---|---|
| _____ | _____ |
| _____ | _____ |
| _____ | _____ |
| _____ | _____ |

*(continues. . .)*

# A Companion Guidebook

Action:                                                           Date Scheduled:

_____                    _____
_____                    _____
_____                    _____
_____                    _____
_____                    _____

- What belief(s) will you program that will assist you to routinely expunge or eliminate guilt? Schedule a date for programming these beliefs.

_____                    _____
_____                    _____
_____                    _____
_____                    _____
_____                    _____

- Consider each person, situation, or act on your list. What are three reasons to forgive yourself for each thing listed?

| _____ | _____ | _____ |
| _____ | _____ | _____ |
| _____ | _____ | _____ |
| _____ | _____ | _____ |
| _____ | _____ | _____ |
| _____ | _____ | _____ |
| _____ | _____ | _____ |

## Puppet or Puppeteer / Dr. Nell Rodgers

- On what date will you take the time to insure that you have forgiven yourself for continuing to feel guilty. Write here about your feelings and actions on that date.

_____
_____
_____
_____
_____
_____
_____

## <u>Guilt Is Searching for Punishment</u>

- What are 3 reasons for eliminating guilt and freeing your mind for more creative and productive thoughts?

| _____ | _____ |
| _____ | _____ |
| _____ | _____ |

- List 3-5 ways you punish yourself.

| _____ | _____ |
| _____ | _____ |
| _____ | _____ |

- Write a belief which overrides your need to punish yourself for each thing on your list. Schedule a date for programming your new beliefs.

| _____ | _____ |
| _____ | _____ |
| _____ | _____ |

# A Companion Guidebook

- Write your personal statement indicating how you will respond to those who "lay guilt trips" on you. Carry this with you and read it daily for one month.

_____
_____
_____

## Now Is All You Have
*(See: On Now, On Fear)*

- List six problems or worries from the past, present, or future you have thought about in the past week.

- What actions can you take today that will put each of these experiences behind you?

- What are five reasons for taking action which keeps you focused on the present moment?

## Puppet or Puppeteer / Dr. Nell Rodgers

- What belief(s) will you program to insure that you are appropriately and positively acting in the present moment? Schedule the date on your calendar for reprogramming.

_____
_____
_____
_____
_____
_____

## Anger Stems From Helplessness
*(See: On Claiming Your Power, On Peace, On Problem Solving, On Self-Disclosure)*

- List the five experiences or situations which excite the greatest amount of anger in you.

_____
_____
_____
_____
_____

- What is making you feel helpless in each of the above instances? Dig down deeply.

_____
_____
_____
_____
_____

# A Companion Guidebook

- What major actions can you take today that will decrease your feelings of helplessness?

　　_____
　　_____

- What three actions can you take within the next 48 hours that will help you feel that you are in control of your life?

　　_____
　　_____
　　_____

- What belief(s) will you program or reprogram that will cause you to feel strong enough to let go of angry outbursts? What will eliminate the helpless feeling? Remember you can only change yourself. Others must change for themselves.

　　_____　　_____
　　_____　　_____

- Schedule dates to reprogram these beliefs.

　　_____　_____　_____　_____　_____

## RESENTMENT REQUIRES COMMITMENT
*(See: On Commitment, On Forgiveness, On Responsibility)*

- Write a minimum of three sentences about each of five major resentments you presently have.

　　_____
　　_____
　　_____

*(continues. . .)*

29

# Puppet or Puppeteer / Dr. Nell Rodgers

- What are three steps you can take to give up your resentment in each instance?

## A Companion Guidebook

- What will happen if you let go of your resentments? Write freely about this using additional sheets of paper or another notebook if needed.

# Puppet or Puppeteer / Dr. Nell Rodgers

*(Continue writing what will happen if you let go of your resentments.)*

- How will other people treat you if they know you no longer hold resentments? Write freely about this using additional sheets of paper or another notebook if needed.

## Puppet or Puppeteer / Dr. Nell Rodgers

*(Continue writing how other people will treat you if you no longer hold resentments.)*

# A COMPANION GUIDEBOOK

## RESENTMENT PUNISHES THE PERSON HOLDING THE RESENTMENT
*(See: On Victimization)*

- What are six ways you are punishing yourself by holding on to resentments?

  _____   _____
  _____   _____
  _____   _____
  _____   _____

- Over the period of one week, write a minimum of one page on each way you have listed. Mornings are best for this activity. Use a separate, dedicated notebook for your additional writings. (They may be destroyed afterwards if you wish.)

## EMOTIONS ARE THE RESULT OF THOUGHTS AND BELIEFS
*(See: On Belief, On Expectations, On Journaling)*

- List those emotions which create the most difficulty for you. Specify the situations most likely to elicit these emotions.

  _____   _____
  _____   _____
  _____   _____
  _____   _____
  _____   _____

- What beliefs are you willing to reprogram in order to shift to more positive emotional responses?

  _____   _____
  _____   _____
  _____   _____
  _____   _____

## PUPPET OR PUPPETEER / DR. NELL RODGERS

- What can you do differently in each of the situations which elicit your most negative emotions?

  _____    _____
  _____    _____
  _____    _____
  _____    _____

- Which five situational experiences will you share with someone whom you trust? When sharing, express difficulties you encounter in the situations and ask for support in making your change to positive responses. Choose a person who will be supporting you. Schedule a date with them to begin your sharing.

  _____    _____
  _____    _____
  _____    _____

## YOU ARE IN CHARGE OF WHAT YOU FEEL (YOUR EMOTIONS)
*(See: On Feeling Emotions, On Being Different, On Getting Support)*

- What three things can you do today to counteract each of your most negative emotions? What can you do to ensure that you enjoy the process?

  _____    _____
  _____    _____
  _____    _____

- What are the easiest three ways you can differently approach or experience *each* situation to eliminate the negatively charged emotion?

  _____    _____    _____
  _____    _____    _____
  _____    _____    _____
  _____    _____    _____

- How will your life be different when you switch to experiencing more positive emotions? Write a page about this.

## Anger and Resentment Keep You Stuck in Victimization

- Holding on to my resentment and anger gives me permission to:

    Write five things. (Dig deeply and get the true reasons.) Example: *While yelling or giving the "silent treatment," I get to feel powerful in relation to my spouse.*

    _____          _____
    _____          _____
    _____

- Write freely about your feeling of superiority in relation to each of the five things.

# A Companion Guidebook

- Write a paragraph about how to eliminate your anger and resentment for each situation.

## You Are Perfect Just the Way You Are
*(See: On Loving Yourself)*

- List the things you most dislike about yourself. Make the effort to stay focused on your acts, beliefs, emotions, responses and those "personality flaws" you think you have.

  _____  _____  _____
  _____  _____  _____
  _____  _____  _____
  _____  _____  _____

- What assets from your outstanding abilities listed in the exercise "You Are Praiseworthy" (page 12) will cancel out each of the things you dislike about yourself? List at least two of your asset(s) beside each of the things you dislike about yourself.

  _____  _____  _____
  _____  _____  _____
  _____  _____  _____
  _____  _____  _____
  _____  _____  _____
  _____  _____  _____

- Which things about your body, such as age, height, big hips or posture, have you believed to be negative or less than perfect? List them. Write a belief(s) which supports you in changing what you can and accepting those which cannot be changed. Reprogram this immediately!

  _____  _____
  _____  _____
  _____  _____
  _____  _____

# A Companion Guidebook

- What actions can you take now to affirm acceptance of yourself? Remember that transformation is a process. These actions will require monitoring.

  _____     _____
  _____     _____
  _____     _____

- When will you take this action? When will you program related belief(s)?

  Action:                     Belief:

  _____     _____
  _____     _____
  _____     _____
  _____     _____

## Results Come From Actions Related to Desires
*(See: On Getting Going, On Problem Solving, On Risk-Taking, On Commitment, On Goals)*

- What three wishes would you make if you knew that today they would magically come true?

  _____     _____
  _____     _____

- What five actions could you take that would be enjoyable and at the same time would take you toward fulfillment of each of these wishes?

  _____     _____
  _____     _____
  _____     _____

## Puppet or Puppeteer / Dr. Nell Rodgers

- Which action will you take tomorrow, within one week, two weeks and three weeks? Consistent and persistent action actualizes goals and desires.

## Self-Disclosure Is Growth
*(See: On Self-Disclosure, On Telling Friends, On Fear)*

- List ten thoughts or behaviors which you feel embarrassed to talk about.

- What can you release today that will promote further love of yourself and your creativity?

- What are three intimate feelings or secrets will you commit to sharing during the next week?

- What limiting beliefs can you reprogram into an affirmative belief which will support self-disclosure and relieve fear? Schedule a date for this reprogramming.

# A Companion Guidebook

## Shame Comes From Within
*(See: On Being Different, On Rules, On Peace, On Drawing)*

- List ten thoughts or behaviors of which you feel ashamed.

  _____   _____   _____
  _____   _____   _____
  _____   _____   _____
  _____   _____   _____

- For each thought or behavior just listed, write down how you can turn the shame around to feel good about yourself. This may take awhile. Keep at it even if you must return during a later session.

# Puppet or Puppeteer / Dr. Nell Rodgers

*(Continue writing how you can turn your shame around to feel good about yourself.)*

# A Companion Guidebook

- What are two beliefs which drive your shame for each of the above thoughts or behaviors?

| Thought/Behavior: | Belief: | Belief: |
|---|---|---|
| _____ | _____ | _____ |
| _____ | _____ | _____ |
| _____ | _____ | _____ |
| _____ | _____ | _____ |
| _____ | _____ | _____ |
| _____ | _____ | _____ |
| _____ | _____ | _____ |
| _____ | _____ | _____ |
| _____ | _____ | _____ |
| _____ | _____ | _____ |
| _____ | _____ | _____ |
| _____ | _____ | _____ |

- Write down your feelings about these beliefs.

_____
_____
_____
_____
_____
_____
_____
_____
_____
_____

# Puppet or Puppeteer / Dr. Nell Rodgers

- Restate each of these beliefs so that shame is eliminated. Commit to making these shifts.

| Belief: | New Statement: | Date to Program: |
| --- | --- | --- |
| _____ | _____ | _____ |
| _____ | _____ | _____ |
| _____ | _____ | _____ |
| _____ | _____ | _____ |
| _____ | _____ | _____ |
| _____ | _____ | _____ |
| _____ | _____ | _____ |
| _____ | _____ | _____ |
| _____ | _____ | _____ |
| _____ | _____ | _____ |

- Write down your feelings about the new beliefs.

_____
_____
_____
_____
_____
_____
_____
_____
_____

- What will it take for you to be pleased with who you are and how you behave in order to eliminate your shame? Write your answer in a minimum of a page.

## Puppet or Puppeteer / Dr. Nell Rodgers

- List 15 reasons to love yourself unconditionally.

_____  _____  _____

_____  _____  _____

_____  _____  _____

_____  _____  _____

_____  _____  _____

## Turn Your Negative Statements Into Positive Statements
*(See: On Expectations, On Failure, On Loving Yourself)*

- List a minimum of eight things or situations you feel the most negative about. Turn each negative statement into a positive statement.

    Example:    *I hate it when people tell me what to do.*
    *I will send love to those who tell me what to do as I make my own informed choices.*

_____

_____

_____

_____

_____

_____

_____

_____

_____

_____

_____

_____

- Write at least 25 negative statements about yourself. Turn each one into a positive statement. This will give you direction and help you to reprogram your thinking into more positive thoughts. Do this exercise on two separate sheets of paper. Write all of the negative statements on a separate sheet outside this book. Write positive statements here. Upon completion, burn the paper with negative statements, letting them go. Keep the positive statements. Refer to them often.

## Puppet or Puppeteer / Dr. Nell Rodgers

### Your Thoughts and Behaviors Determine Your Skills and Excellence

• List five areas in your life that you believe to be less than perfect.

_____  _____  _____

_____  _____

• What are you willing to do today to make each thing on your list the way you want it to be?

_____  _____

_____  _____

_____  _____

_____

• What belief(s) can you change and/or reprogram which will take you toward your desires as you give up the need for perfection? Write at least four.

_____  _____

_____  _____

• What would happen if you gave up your need for perfection? Write freely about this.

*(Continue writing what would happen if you gave up your need for perfection.)*

# Puppet or Puppeteer / Dr. Nell Rodgers

- How can you eliminate your fears associated with giving up your perfectionistic tendencies. Write two pages about how to eliminate these fears.

# A Companion Guidebook

*(Continue writing on giving up your perfectionistic tendencies.)*

# Puppet or Puppeteer / Dr. Nell Rodgers

## Martyrdom Is Certain Doom
*(See: On Decisions, On Double Messages, On Gratitude, On Risk Taking, On Victim)*

• List three things you have denied yourself or believe others have kept you from having. How?

_____        _____
_____        _____
_____        _____
_____        _____
_____        _____

• What are ten martyred behaviors you can eliminate now? What are ten self denials? Write the personal cost(s) beside each of these behaviors. Some will have several costs.

    Example:
    *I always cook for relatives on holidays.*   *I don't get to enjoy my family as much.*
                                                            *My budget is really stretched beyond limits.*

_____        _____
_____        _____
_____        _____
_____        _____
_____        _____
_____        _____
_____        _____
_____        _____
_____        _____
_____        _____

# A Companion Guidebook

- Write two pages about what your payoff is for maintaining your martyred behavior.

    Example: *"I get to feel self-righteous and better than others who do less or never give of themselves."*

# Puppet or Puppeteer / Dr. Nell Rodgers

*(Continue writing what your payoff is for maintaining your martyred behavior.)*

- How can you reward yourself daily for your willingness to evolve into the magnificent being that you are? Make the rewards high enough to motivate your change. Fill this page.

# Puppet or Puppeteer / Dr. Nell Rodgers

- Compare your notes on these last two exercises. Use the information to complete the next two exercises.

## **Rewarding Yourself Is Motivating**
*(See: On Motivation, On Commitment)*

- List a minimum of three rewards you will give yourself weekly for the next six weeks.

_____    _____    _____

_____    _____    _____

- List the action(s) you will take which, when taken, will merit a self reward.

_____    _____    _____

_____    _____    _____

_____    _____    _____

## **Feelings Are Your Barometer**
*(See: On Feeling Emotions, On Peace, On Self-Disclosure, On Vulnerability)*

- List ten feelings you would rather not experience.

_____    _____    _____

_____    _____    _____

_____    _____    _____

_____    _____    _____

- How can you most easily uncover the beliefs which cause you to avoid these feelings while at the same time learning to honor all your feelings? Write a minimum of one page.

## Puppet or Puppeteer / Dr. Nell Rodgers

• Which uncomfortable feeling(s) are you willing to reveal to a trusted friend when next you experience it? Write at least two. List the friend(s). Schedule a time with each person to share.

_____  _____  _____

_____  _____  _____

_____  _____  _____

_____  _____  _____

• The more you authentically reveal yourself, the greater your self-esteem and evolution. On separate paper, write as much as you need to in order to reconcile at least two of the ten feelings. Come back to this exercise periodically and continue until you have written about all ten items on you list. List each feeling which has been reconciled as a reminder.

_____  _____  _____

_____  _____  _____

_____  _____  _____

_____  _____  _____

## Power Originates From Within
*(See: On Claiming Your Power, On Vulnerability, On Attachment)*

• List five times when you have felt or now feel powerless.

_____  _____

_____  _____

_____  _____

# A Companion Guidebook

- What six things can you do (or could you have done) in each of these situations that would have created a feeling of being empowered?

_____  _____  _____

- What are your non-supportive beliefs that keep you from your power?

_____  _____

- What beliefs can you program to counter each of these beliefs?

_____  _____

## Puppet or Puppeteer / Dr. Nell Rodgers

- What are your negative belief(s) and feelings about people who seem too powerful?

_____          _____

_____          _____

- What part of yourself is mirrored in these negative belief(s) and feelings? Write a minimum of a page about these parts of yourself.

## A Companion Guidebook

- Write a page on the difference between power and overpowering. Include words such as force, domineering, control, overbearing, authoritative, integrity and "taking a stand".

## Puppet or Puppeteer / Dr. Nell Rodgers

# Living With Purpose Creates Fullness of Life
*(See: On Getting Going, On Motivation, On Intuition)*

- *My purpose in life is...* Write it out. If you think you do not know, "make it up" now and come back to this point after more of these introspective exercises are completed or when you realize what it is. Ask yourself repeatedly, "What is my purpose in life?" This is an excellent question to take into meditation/relaxation. Purpose can be, and often is, quite simple and ordinary, such as modeling responsible, loving behavior.

  _____
  _____
  _____
  _____

- What three actions can you take to move further into your purpose?

  _____   _____
  _____   _____

- On what date will you take the first action? Schedule the date in your calendar.

- Which beliefs cause you to veer off purpose or neglect pursuit of your purpose?

  _____   _____   _____
  _____   _____   _____

- Is it true that you are already living your purpose? Write a page about this. Write a second page about honoring yourself and your purpose.

# A Companion Guidebook

*(Continue writing on how you are already living your purpose.)*

## Puppet or Puppeteer / Dr. Nell Rodgers

*(Continue writing about honoring yourself and your purpose.)*

# A Companion Guidebook

## Expressing Gratitude Is Healing

- List a minimum of 50 things for which you feel grateful.

## Puppet or Puppeteer / Dr. Nell Rodgers

- Write at least one page about how you felt after creating this list.

# A Companion Guidebook

## Needing Permission Sets up a Child/Parent Relationship Which Disallows Evolved Behavior
*(See: On Attachment, On Fear, On Freedom, On Internal vs External Control)*

- List a minimum of ten things or behaviors you never give yourself permission to have or do.

_____  _____  _____

_____  _____  _____

_____  _____  _____

_____  _____  _____

- What six specific things can you do that will change your immature or ineffective behaviors into responsible, mature behaviors?

_____  _____

_____  _____

_____  _____

- What belief(s) cause you to act as if you need permission to be yourself? Write at least six. What new empowering beliefs can you program that will support individual, responsible, mature behavior? Schedule a time for programming.

_____  _____

_____  _____

_____  _____

_____  _____

# Puppet or Puppeteer / Dr. Nell Rodgers

## Love of Self Comes From the Self

- Make a list of the things and people you love.

| | | |
|---|---|---|
| _____ | _____ | _____ |
| _____ | _____ | _____ |
| _____ | _____ | _____ |
| _____ | _____ | _____ |
| _____ | _____ | _____ |
| _____ | _____ | _____ |
| _____ | _____ | _____ |
| _____ | _____ | _____ |

- On separate paper, write a 2-3 page letter to yourself explaining why you are worthy and deserving of these things. Mail the letter to yourself and read it when it arrives.

- The next day, write a second letter to yourself explaining the many reasons your friends love you. Mail the letter to yourself and read it when it arrives.

- On the following day, write a love letter to yourself. Mail the letter to yourself and read it when it arrives.

## Create a Private Magic Zone in Your Mind
*(See: Chapters 4 & 5)*

- Routinely use a private personal zone as a retreat to quietly ask for direction in your life or to quiet yourself when stressed or frustrated. Schedule a date to create this space and specific times in your day to enjoy it.

## A Companion Guidebook

### Play Brings Magic, Healing and Joy to Life
*(See: On Play, On Laughter, On Flexibility)*

- Make a work: play: work: play: work: play schedule. Then do it! Post your schedule in a conspicuous place and commit to following through.

- List activities of play that you enjoy. Write down the dates you will do each within the next 30 days. Be certain to include silliness such as coloring outside the lines of a coloring book or giggling with friends. Hug trees, sing to a star, play hopscotch with children, splash a puddle.

_____    _____
_____    _____
_____    _____
_____    _____
_____    _____
_____    _____
_____    _____
_____    _____
_____    _____
_____    _____
_____    _____
_____    _____
_____    _____
_____    _____
_____    _____
_____    _____
_____    _____
_____    _____
_____    _____
_____    _____

**Puppet or Puppeteer / Dr. Nell Rodgers**

## Stretching Your Limits Is a Way to Grow and Transform

- Write two pages about how you limit yourself. Make decisions about potential changes.

# A Companion Guidebook

*(Continue writing on how you limit yourself and your decisions about potential changes.)*

# Puppet or Puppeteer / Dr. Nell Rodgers

- List five areas of your life in which you would like to grow.

  _____    _____    _____
  _____    _____    _____
  _____    _____    _____
  _____    _____    _____

- Write about each area above in which you talk about how you can stretch your limits in that area. Go beyond what you are usually comfortable doing. This is about getting out of your box.

# A Companion Guidebook

- Do something each week to stretch your beliefs, your behavior, your love limits, your forgiveness limits or any other limit you have set for yourself. Write a paragraph about your progress the following week.

_____

_____

_____

_____

_____

## Routine Assessment and Monitoring Lets You Know Where You Are Now and Where You Are Headed

- Use this exercise to regularly update knowledge of your limiting beliefs and schedule reprogramming. Also, use it to determine where and when you need to install new or different empowering beliefs. Refer to the above exercises and repeat them using these monitoring activities when desired or appropriate. Watch your progress.

    1. Which belief(s) limits you the most at this time? Set a date to reprogram these belief(s) into supportive belief(s).

2. What three things do you want most in your life at this time? What are the belief(s) which would support your getting these desires? Write out the beliefs, schedule time and program them.

_____   _____
_____   _____
_____   _____
_____   _____
_____   _____

- Which is the most empowering belief to reprogram right now? Set a date and program this empowering belief(s).

_____
_____

3. What are three ways you can systematically and routinely keep awareness of this newly programmed belief?

_____   _____
_____   _____

4. What two actions can you take for each desire/goal listed in number two above that will move you toward them now?

_____   _____   _____
_____   _____   _____
_____   _____   _____
_____   _____   _____
_____   _____   _____
_____   _____   _____

- Write out in narrative form why each action is needed, where it will take you, whether you need further action, how and when you will take action, and dates the action will be taken.

# Puppet or Puppeteer / Dr. Nell Rodgers

## Specific Circumstances Call for Explicit Decisions

- Use this exercise to dig deeper into who you are or to uncover feelings and make decisions related to specific circumstances in your life. The protocol is applicable to any situation.

Here, the exercise is written with body weight as the problem topic. Those words in *italics* are to be changed to the appropriate words which fit your circumstance. The framework for other applications is in regular type. Remember to refer to Section II of *Puppet or Puppeteer* for related information. For example, in looking at excess body weight you might refer to On Attachment, On Claiming Your Power, On Commitment, On Diet, On Exercise, On Feeling, On Health and Wellness, On Nutrition, On Problem Solving, On Setbacks and so forth, using all that you think apply to your specific circumstance.

Complete this form with appropriate statements about your problem area. Write a page about each statement. You may wish to copy or rewrite these 14 items.

- What are my payoffs for *weighing* "x" instead of my desired *weight* of "x"?

- What are my most unpleasant thoughts about *my body*?

- What am I most often angry about when dealing with my *excess weight*?

- What are at least six reasons I carry my *excess weight of "x" pounds*?

- What is the action, trait, situation or behavior I have not yet forgiven in myself or others which helps perpetuate carrying my *excess weight of "x" pounds*?

- What can I do now to responsibly accept the situation as it is while preparing for action to change the situation to that which I desire?

- Is there an unconscious or conscious belief(s) I need to change that will get me unstuck from my present position of *carrying "x" excess pounds*?

- What are three steps I can take today to begin the process of *eliminating my excess weight*?

- What is the best affirmation(s) I can now use to acknowledge and claim the positive aspects of *my body as it is?*

- What belief(s), when reprogrammed, will assist me most to achieve my *desired weight of "x"*?

- What are ten pleasures I can choose to enjoy (*instead of eating*) when I feel compelled to *overeat*?

- What key word can I use in the moment I am choosing to *overeat* to remind myself that I have a choice about *overeating*?

## A Companion Guidebook

- What ten behaviors and/or actions will help me to love myself more instead of *overeating?*

- What ten things can I do which will allow others to love me more?

- Schedule a specific date in your calendar for review and modification (if needed) of this plan.

## **Resolute Principles and Values Are Your Governing Force**

- The principle(s) and values(s) by which I choose to live my life are... Write them out.

This information is like a mission statement for your life. Take lots of time with it. Perhaps write 7-8 pages, then reduce the data to the main points on one sheet. Be very specific. You can always rearrange the information by removing or adding material which is reflective of your most current thinking. Schedule a date for completion as well as dates for review. Record the main points here.

# Puppet or Puppeteer / Dr. Nell Rodgers

## Your Life Is Declaration of Your Beliefs

- Write your own obituary.

    1. Start with that for which you think you will be <u>most</u> remembered.

    _____
    _____

    2. Next write about that for which you would <u>like</u> to be remembered.

    _____
    _____

    3. Write your obituary as it would appear now, assuming you do nothing different in your life.

    _____
    _____

    4. What are five actions you can take that will cause you to invest energy and time in doing that for which you would like to be remembered?

    _____        _____
    _____        _____
    _____        _____
    _____

    5. Write your obituary as it would appear assuming that you take these five action steps.

    _____
    _____

- Set a date for an annual review of your own obituary. Mark it in your calendar each year.

## An Integrity Inventory Will Reflect Your Self-Worth
*(See: On Integrity, On Victim, On Failure, On Loving Yourself)*

• Take an integrity inventory by listing the areas of your life in which you sacrifice(ed) your integrity; work, spiritual, relationships, actions taken, play, finances and so forth.

1. What one thing can I do today that will bring me closer to personal integrity?

   _____

2. What are three things I can do to bring my integrity into balance with my values?

   _____   _____   _____

3. What core belief can I program which will enable me to live with integrity?

   _____

4. What three activities bring me the greatest feelings of self-worth and importance?

   _____   _____   _____

5. How can I make certain that I schedule at least one of these activities daily?

   _____   _____

   _____   _____

   _____   _____

6. An additional part of this exercise can be added. Review your life in 5-10 year segments. List what brought you happiness and joy. Look at what brought you disappointment and frustration. Note your level of integrity during each situation. Write each segment and the corresponding information separately.

# Puppet or Puppeteer / Dr. Nell Rodgers

- Write a minimum of one page about your current level of integrity.

# A COMPANION GUIDEBOOK

## REVIEWING WHERE YOU ARE CAN OPEN NEW DOORS

Create time in your schedule at least every six months to answer the following questions in writing. The answers will help clarify your continuing purpose and refine your goals of personal growth.

1. What am I the most afraid of admitting?

2. What do I love about myself today?

3. What things, if any, are holding me back?

4. What am I most shy about?

5. What do I still dream about doing in my life?

6. What do I most often fantasize about?

7. What would I do if I had plenty of money, the loving support of others, and knew that I would succeed?

8. What would I most regret not having done if my life ended today?

- Write a minimum of two or three pages which discuss the answers to each of the questions one through eight. Make decisions which are appropriate and desired.

# Puppet or Puppeteer / Dr. Nell Rodgers

*(Continue writing answers to questions one through eight.)*

## A Companion Guidebook

*(Continue writing answers to questions one through eight.)*

# Puppet or Puppeteer / Dr. Nell Rodgers

## Expanded Thinking Decreases Angst

These thoughts are for your consideration on a daily basis. Add your own similar thoughts. Carry a small notebook for review and additions.

- People never abuse that which they think is valuable. Love and value yourself.

- Opinions are of little value. Reinforce opinions with values. Reinforce values with action.

- Generally avoid following the advice of others except in a professional capacity.

- Repetition builds confidence. What are you repeating? Does it reflect your values? Is it self-empowering?

- Reward yourself. Pain is the *other* motivator. You have a choice.

- Cherish diversity.

## Giving Yourself Permission Is Vital To a Full and Fulfilling Life

- This exercise will bring you closer to freedom and choice in your everyday life. We often imprison ourselves because we fail to give ourselves permission to be or do.

    1. Write down your top five experiences, worries, fears, concerns, circumstances, situations, etc., which are now creating or have, in the past, resulted in negative feelings inside yourself.

    _____    _____

    _____    _____

    _____

    2. Work with each of the five things independently. Write out a specific issue from number one. Divide a piece of paper into halves by drawing a line down the middle. Underneath the issue, on the left side, list ALL the very worst things you can think of which might happen in relation to that issue.

    3. On the right side of the paper, list any justification that you can imagine for your worry or concern in relation to each of the statements.

## A COMPANION GUIDEBOOK

4. Mentally weigh each item in both columns. Use integrity. If the justification in the right side is *valid* regarding your concerns listed on the left side, write true in the right column. Write false if it is invalid.

Example: (Use the list you created) I worry about people thinking I dress too casually at work.

| | |
|---|---|
| *People will laugh at me.* | *Everyone else dresses up more — False, not everyone.* |
| *I will get stared at.* | *People look at me all the time — False, they're too busy worrying about themselves. Some will stare. True* |
| *People will think I don't care.* | *People say we should dress properly — True. Almost everyone talks about how caring I am. True.* |
| *My spouse judges me.* | *I fear this is true — False. My fear is unjustifiable.* |

5. Define two actions you can take to alter the outcome of each item which has been labeled "true". Forget those which are false and move on with your life.

6. List three things can you do to give yourself permission to stop negatively obsessing about the outcome of each of the things listed which have no justifiable reason for concern or worry.

7. Which of the potential outcomes give you the most discomfort?

_____   _____

_____   _____

_____   _____

## PUPPET OR PUPPETEER / DR. NELL RODGERS

• Which beliefs do you need to reprogram to avoid this discomfort?

• Give yourself permission to change your behavior and response(s). List specific responses which would permit you to respond with integrity while enhancing your personal power.

_____     _____
_____     _____
_____     _____

## KNOWING WHERE YOU ARE OPTIMIZES POTENTIAL FOR CHANGE

• This exercise, when complete, will reflect those areas of your life which are currently needing work, or which you are working to change. Repeat the exercise periodically.

1. List the two people in your life with whom you get the angriest.

_____     _____

2. What do these people do that makes you the most angry?

_____
_____

3. What do you most dislike in other people's behavior?

_____     _____
_____     _____

4. What types of situations upset you the most?

_____     _____
_____     _____
_____     _____

# A Companion Guidebook

5. Describe in detail 4-5 things/situations which you intensely dislike or abhor.

_____
_____
_____
_____
_____
_____

6. What makes you the most angry about yourself or your own behavior?

_____
_____

- Look at your answers. These answers will show you what you do not yet forgive. They reflect what you are working on spiritually at this point in your life.

- Use any of the personal reflective exercises to enhance your desired changes. Write a couple of paragraphs about each thing you choose.

## SHIFTING FROM NEGATIVE TO POSITIVE SELF-TALK IS EMPOWERING

- Look at your negative self-talk. Be expansive in your search for negative self-talk. Write down as many statements as you can. Use the following positive restatement examples to then rephrase your own written negative statements. Make all of your statements positive.

1. Someday I'm going to ask for a raise. I deserve it.

    *My work is valuable. I am an asset to this company. I will ask for a raise before (set date).*

2. They just keep adding more work when I finish up quickly, so why work so hard?

*(continues. . .)*

# Puppet or Puppeteer / Dr. Nell Rodgers

> *When I finish my work quickly, I feel great and have an opportunity to do more, demonstrating my skills and providing data to support a promotion and a raise in salary.*

3. It's too late to start anything in only 15 minutes.

   > *Wow! I have 15 minutes to spend frugally. I know that even a small start on the next project puts me ahead.*

4. Maybe somebody else will finish this if I postpone it long enough.

   > *By completing this now, I will feel better about myself and create another opportunity to be trustworthy with the tasks I am given.*

5. Maybe the pain will go away if I just wait a couple of days.

   > *I know that pain is my body's way of telling me something is wrong. I cherish my health; therefore, I will call for an appointment to have it checked now.*

6. The boss doesn't really care about when this gets done, so I'll do it when I get around to it.

   > *Although the boss does not seem to need this now, I will get it done so that I can eliminate the nagging thought that it is still waiting to be done and at the same time free my energy for more exciting tasks. My boss may notice my efficiency, too.*

7. I'll quit smoking (overeating, overindulging, overspending) or begin exercising (eating nutritional foods, getting proper rest, saving for emergencies or investment) as soon as I _____.

   > *Now is all that I have and the most important time to do anything is at this time. I love myself and care about my health enough to begin my program now.*

8. It's not due until week after next, so I'll wait a couple of days to begin.

   > *The faster I get this done, the faster I will continue to become habitually effective in being more efficient and enhancing my self-esteem and personal growth.*

9. I meant to get that done, but I forgot it.

   > *I like getting tasks accomplished quickly. Therefore, I always keep a notepad to assist me in assessing what is to be done and in establishing priorities.*

- Use this exercise at least every six months to review, uncover and eliminate negative self-talk.

# A Companion Guidebook

*(Rephrase your own written negative stataements here.)*

# Puppet or Puppeteer / Dr. Nell Rodgers

## Disengaging From the Past Facilitates Increased Knowledge of, and Engagement With the Present

• Important experiences or events may negatively or positively impact our lives. Sometimes we unconsciously record or cling to emotional responses which continue to affect us for a long time. These events can be yet another way in which we are programmed to automatically respond instead of making a conscious choice. Here is a list of some events which may evoke emotionally significant responses. (See: NET, Chapter 4 in *Puppet or Puppeteer*)

| | | |
|---|---|---|
| Birth | High School | Peer Acceptance in High School |
| Birth of Siblings | Illness | Learning of a Morbid Diagnosis |
| Bottle Weaning | Accidents | Death of a Loved One |
| Toilet Training | Surgery | Separation From a Loved One |
| Perceived Abandonment | Parental Conflict | Religious Experiences |
| Death of a Pet | Parental Divorce | Baby-sitters |
| Beginning School | Tax Investigation | Graduation High School |
| Significant Teachers | Abortion | Fire |
| Peer Relationships | Attending College | Any Personal Tragedy |
| Praise or Punishment | Financial Disruptions | Failed Marriage |
| Onset of Puberty | Romantic Failure | Loss of Possessions |
| Wedding | Job Failure or Loss | Onset of Sexual Relationships |
| Fights | Legal Problems | Career Changes |
| Romances | Illness of a Loved One | Sexual Conflicts |

• Which of these have you experienced? Are there other significant emotional events in your life?

• Rate each experience as positive or negative.

• What is at least one guiding belief you can relate to each event? Write them out individually.

Example:

*Significant Teacher - Positive. My second-grade teacher loved me. I learned to spell exceptionally well in order to please her so she would continue to love me. I got a prize for being the best speller in my school. I now believe that if I am really good or do a good job I will be rewarded.*

*Significant Teacher - Negative. My eleventh-grade teacher disliked me and was also very rigid with the students. I "covered" being fat by being comical. She told me people were laughing at me and not with me. I started believing that I was a misfit.*

## A Companion Guidebook

- Which of these beliefs *currently* are a part of who you are? Which do you wish to reprogram or eliminate?

  _____    _____
  _____    _____
  _____    _____
  _____    _____
  _____    _____

- Are you willing to commit and follow through on your commitment to resolve the charges on emotionally significant events as they occur? Write an affirmation that will confirm this.

  _____
  _____

## CLICHÉ – BELIEFS CAN BE MISLEADING AND SELF-DEFEATING

- Change the following limiting truisms into more powerful beliefs. This exercise will give you practice in identifying, acknowledging and restating your own beliefs. After changing the beliefs given here, identify and convert your own personal cliché – beliefs.

  1. *I'm poor but honest.* There is no connection between these two things. You can be rich and have total honesty and integrity. You can be quite dishonest and very poor.

     *Rewritten Example: I am honest. I have integrity. I am rich in every way. I have all the money I need. Money easily flows to me.*

  2. *It's only my opinion.* The inference is that your opinion is less than valuable or invalid. The truth is that your opinion is as valuable as anyone else's opinion.

  _____
  _____

*(continues. . .)*

3. *Show-offs are reprehensible.* Talents are valuable. Displaying, sharing or talking about your talents is appropriate. The way in which you do that is fundamental to your acceptance both by yourself and by others.

4. *You don't have what it takes.* "It" takes only desire, determination, commitment and persistence. However, you must be willing.

5. *Money can't buy happiness.* This is true. However, the inference that money is the cause of the happiness in those who do not have it or the cause of unhappiness in those who have lots of it is untrue. Happiness is an inside thing and is unrelated to money.

6. *Everything comes to those who wait.* There is no basis in truth for this statement. To get what you want, you must take action.

7. *Money is the root of all evil.* This quote is attributed to the Bible. However, the actual quote is "the *love* of money" is the root of all evil. When you love yourself, follow your dreams and take action, you will discover and enjoy grace and honesty as well as have money. To love money more than yourself or others can bring evil.

*(continues. . .)*

8. *All good things must come to an end.* There are two ways to look at this statement. *Everything* comes to an end because change is inevitable so make the most of now; good things can be made even better. The second inference is that it is useless to do anything because it will be short-lived. If you have experienced something wonderful, you can do so again. Set up another circumstance.

_____

_____

- You may choose to reprogram some or all of your newly composed beliefs. Set completion dates.

## WHAT YOU SEE MAY BE WHAT YOU WANT TO BELIEVE

Your environment has a powerful impact on your life. Signs, slogans, pictures, mottos and posters can indicate what you believe or wish to believe. Increasing your awareness about your surroundings can help you determine where you may be stuck, what changes you may wish to make, or assist you in creating a more nuturing and self-promoting space.

1. Carefully observe your environment at work, at home, in your automobile (if appropriate) and at any other place where you spend a great deal of time.

2. On a pad, make headings for two columns. One column is labeled as "Motivating, Positive, Nurturing, Warm." The other column is labeled "Non-nurturing, Negative, Sad, Non-motivating."

3. Take the pad and pen to each slogan, sign or picture. Look at each one until you experience a feeling inside yourself. Place the name of that item in the column according to the way it makes you feel.

4. Remove those items from your space which are listed in the non-nurturing column.

5. Get congruent with (reprogram) beliefs which support each statement or picture which you want to be true in your life. (Those in the positive column.)

- Consider this thought. If you already *knew* your signs and slogans to be *true*, would you need them hanging as a reminder?

## PUPPET OR PUPPETEER / DR. NELL RODGERS

## GRATITUDE CULTIVATES CONTENTMENT, GIVING ENGENDERS SELF-LOVE

Use this exercise when you are having difficulty valuing who you are.

- List 30 things for which you are grateful. Oprah Winfrey suggests keeping a gratitude journal in which you write 3-5 things each night which you are grateful for that day.

_____    _____    _____
_____    _____    _____
_____    _____    _____
_____    _____    _____
_____    _____    _____
_____    _____    _____
_____    _____    _____
_____    _____    _____
_____    _____    _____
_____    _____    _____

- Ask yourself this question: What can I do to give to others today? Write down a minimum of four answers and take action on at least one.

_____     _____
_____     _____
_____     _____

- Find a volunteer program that has meaning for you and GET INVOLVED!

- Write two or three letters of thanks to people who have given meaning to your life or otherwise gifted you in some way. Mail them immediately.

- Write a letter of appreciation to a minimum of three family members with whom you have had negative experiences, and thank them for having been in your life. Leave out the negative!

- Write a letter to yourself in which you express appreciation to yourself for having made mistakes that enabled you to learn and grow.

# A Companion Guidebook

- Ask three friends to share what they like most about you. Name them here.

_____   _____   _____

- Program a new belief which supports the loving and nurturing of yourself.

_____

## Your Behavior Reflects Your Self-Judgment

Examine this list to determine the areas in which your beliefs and subsequent behaviors are holding you hostage. Write new beliefs and affirmations which will transform the observed behavior into desirable outcomes. You may also decide to uncover other areas or feelings which might be added to this list. This is but an example.

| Action to Watch or Recently Done | Desirable Outcome or Possible Action |
|---|---|
| Gossip | Speak Positively |
| Think About | Take Action |
| Hearing Words Spoken | Listen/Understand |
| Judging | Observing to Understand |
| Lack of Touch | Feel/Connect/Contact |
| Exist | Live |
| React | Respond |
| Tolerate | Love |
| Anger | Calm Assessment |
| Fear | Courage |
| Needing | Choosing |
| Greed | Gratitude |
| Jealously | Loyalty/Love |
| Hate | Love |
| Revenge | Forgiveness |
| Depression | Giving/Taking Action |
| Worry | Action |
| Criticism | Self-Improvement/Helping Hand |
| Holding On | Releasing |

## Following Through on Commitments Is the Path to Obtaining Goals

This exercise will enable you to consistently bring action for follow-through on commitments, will amplify your desires, and will help you obtain goals.

- What belief(s) or situations keep me from committing myself to changes that will increase pleasure in my life?

  _____  _____
  _____  _____
  _____  _____

- What new belief(s) can be programmed to support me as I make commitments and take actions to create positive changes in my life?

  _____  _____
  _____  _____
  _____  _____

- What are the next five aspirations, goals, choices, wishes or objectives I wish to pursue?

  _____  _____
  _____  _____
  _____  _____

- Of these five, which is the first priority? The second priority? The third priority? The fourth and fifth priorities? If goals are time-sensitive, they may need to go near the top of your list.

  _____  _____
  _____  _____
  _____  _____
  _____  _____
  _____  _____

# A Companion Guidebook

- What action(s) can I take today to begin moving toward my top priority goal? Do my beliefs support me in taking this action? If not, list and reprogram those which limit you.

  _____     _____

  _____     _____

  _____     _____

- List actions to be taken, and the intervals at which they will be taken to obtain your two top priorities. When one goal is reached, move the next priority up to number two and begin taking action on that objective. When down to the last two on your list, add more goals to your list and continue with this process. You may wish to use a special notebook for this process.

Each morning stand in front of a mirror and make these statements as you look at yourself.

> _(Your name)_, I love you.
>
> What can I, _(your name)_, do today that will bring me joy?
>
> What can I, _(your name)_, do today that will move me closer to my goal of _(top priority)_?
>
> Listen for the answers and take the necessary action.

## FEEDING YOUR SPIRIT IS ITS OWN REWARD

Everyone needs nurturing and to have their spirit fed. Doing so brings balance and stability, creativity and inner clarity. Use this exercise to feed your spirit.

- Reserve a space somewhere in your home that is used only for quiet times. You may place items with special meaning or value there to remind yourself to listen to your special inner voice when using this space. Schedule time to visit this space as well as using it spontaneously when needed.

- Make absolutely certain that you get three balanced meals and 6-8 glasses of water daily.

- Let go of the past by decision, reprogramming and/or forming new habits.

- Take time to meditate or sit in silence a minimum of 15-20 minutes daily. Use your quiet space.

- Schedule a weekly time for assessing and reprogramming your beliefs.

_(continues. . .)_

# Puppet or Puppeteer / Dr. Nell Rodgers

- Project abundance thinking. Giving is *always* returned many times over what is given. Even if you think you cannot afford to give money, give some anyway. Clinging to your money or possessions reaps little, if any, reward. Start programming yourself in every way you can imagine, to know that there is enough—enough money, enough food, enough clothes, enough everything!

- Take time on a regular basis, perhaps every 6-12 months to reexamine your values and principles. Your inner work may have caused them to shift. If so, do they now conflict with other, older values? What will you do to align your conflicting subconscious beliefs with your new conscious values and principles?

- Focus on whatever you are doing at any given moment. Lack of full attention to any task, exercise or play can rob you of the full benefits or cause you to do less than your best.

- Make a commitment and take the time to venture into different experiences, events and friendly relationships.

- Explore your creativity. Everyone has it. What is your expression of creativity that most exhilarates you? Find a way to express that! Even the smallest expression will lift your spirit.

- Do something nice for someone or some group every day. Bake bread for a shut-in, sing for nursing home residents, invite friends over to bake cookies for the orphanage children, or call a friend who is experiencing a rough time. Write a special note to someone.

- Make a decision to learn something new every single day. Use your mind or lose its agility.

- Do something to stretch your thinking at least every 6-8 months. Old habits are stagnating.

- Resolve to have daily laughter. Laughter is among the most powerful of healers.

- Recognize that you have impact on everyone you meet. Inspect your impressions, reactions, interactions, judgments, and actions. Determine if you have left the imprint(s) you desired to leave with others.

- Place yourself in the presence of friends, mentors, acquaintances and so forth whom you trust and admire. Energy and spirit are drained by negative people and situations.

## A Companion Guidebook

## __Giving Permission Means Something Is Authorized and Sanctioned__

Make a list of all the things you want to do. Remind yourself that you have the power to grant yourself permission to do them. Keep the list handy for reference. Post it where it can be seen.

Here is a sample list. It is not exhaustive.

I <u>(Your name)</u> give myself permission to:

- Glow
- Sing
- Teach
- Say no
- Hug trees
- Play in mud
- Have abundance
- Be totally healthy
- Cry during movies
- Relish my successes
- Take time for myself
- Take life LESS "seriously"
- Challenge my own beliefs
- Take dancing lessons
- Enjoy life, work and play
- Yell with delight during fireworks
- Love myself with my whole heart
- Read faster and comprehend more
- See and experience myself as wonderful
- Have a growing awareness of myself and others
- Give to others out of an abundance consciousness
- Experience my potential even if I have setbacks along the way
- Eat pomegranates in or out of season (Or any other special food)

## I Am Free to Be My Authentic Self at All Times!

# Pulling Your Own Strings
## Requires Clarity and Personal Focus

We have established that personal power comes from within. The word chakra means "centers of energy" and serves to help us focus on the most concentrated energy forces in our body. We can experience our power when least expected and know the surprise of, "Hey, that was great!" We can be embarrassed by lack of personal power when we "cave" or acquiesce. We can use our power to move straight forward into action or to restrain reactions and unrewarding activities. Gaining awareness of who we are and feeding the energy centers of our bodies can provide entry and connection to the power center which resides within each of us. The following exercises and activities are guidelines designed to assist you in designing your own personal path of unfolding. A more extensive and detailed explanation of each chakra's governing activities and associated results in the body is presented in *Puppet or Puppeteer: Choose the Life You Want to Live,* Section I, Chapter 5. (I highly encourage you to read that chapter before using this section of the companion guidebook.)

*"What lies behind us and what lies before us are tiny matters compared to what lies within us."*
Ralph Waldo Emerson

*"You can't depend on your judgement when your imagination is out of focus."*
Mark Twain

# Puppet or Puppeteer / Dr. Nell Rodgers

Quieting the mind through focused relaxation is a simple and forthright way of keeping our energy centers fluid and open. The result is that we remain more connected with our thoughts, dreams and desired responses. We are then capable of directing instead of reacting to life. By daily taking a few minutes for quiet time, pent-up emotions and misconceptions can be released. Physical energy is actually increased. The mind becomes focused and sharp, ready to assist and support us in whatever we are planning or doing. Quieting the mind also provides awareness and is a means for programming new data, including your desired automatic responses within the subconscious. Remember that this procedure is called by several names; Meditation, Relaxation Response, Alpha Relaxation, focused attention and many other labels. The name of the process is immaterial. The important thing is to routinely engage in quieting the chatter of your mind; to eliminate negative self-talk; to connect with your deepest self; to "install" your own programs instead of those which were given to you early in life.

If you are one of the few people who fear meditation, please be assured that there is nothing to fear. Meditative relaxation is scientifically based. There is nothing "hokey" nor anti-anything. You are merely allowing the energies of your body to come into balance. As this happens, your body's operating systems are enhanced. The "yamma-yamma" of your mind is quieted, thus allowing you the opportunity to focus on goals, solutions and any healing that you might want— physical, relationships, financial stress and so forth. If you feel uneasy or awkward in the beginning, stick with it. Some of the language may seem uncomfortable at first. This is not unusual and you are not in any way being judged. This a not a competitive activity. You are not striving for perfection, but rather the opposite. You are allowing yourself to be fully present and aware of your thoughts. It is for you alone to experience as you wish.

In the following exercises you will focus on the colors and energy forces at each chakra (energy center) level. As noted, chapter five in *Puppet or Puppeteer* details each center and the associated organs of the body. There you will also find the functions and emotions related to each center. You are shown the areas of the body which are affected by each center, along with the related colors and sounds associated with each. For example, the sound associated with the fourth center is "ahhhhhh." The heart, lungs, immune and endocrine systems are governed here. Thus, the very important functions of breathing, healing and regulatory function sit here. Some associated emotions are grief, yearning, joy, vulnerability, dogma and harmony. As you progress with meditative relaxation, you will further understand its value and the advantages of quieting your mind. The intent in these specific exercises will be revealed as you engage in the process. Your body will automatically support your efforts. It wants the balance you providing.

There are exercises for each energy center along with step-by-step guidance for each practice. They do require a place of quietness where you will be uninterrupted. The greater your focus, the more dynamic your results. Ignore or unplug the telephone. Close the door to family or friends. Refuse messages. Dare anyone to interrupt! Do whatever you must do to establish an area of comfort and peaceful calm. A necessary first step in tapping into your inner power is taking responsibility to create a space in which it can be manifest, understood and utilized. Visualization is a vital aspect of each exercise. If you believe you have difficulty in visualizing go back and read Chapter 4 of *Puppet or Puppeteer: Choose the Life You Want to Live* again. Remember, if you can think of Santa Claus and know the color of his suit, you can visualize. The colors and visualizations are a primary force in these exercises. However, the addition of tones and sounds as indicated will enhance any meditation at any level. For instance the fourth center sound is ahhhhh. Actually making the sound of ahhhhh as you vividly hold the visualization in your mind will create a more powerful experience for you. Since the heart and lungs are associated with this center, sending the sound and the energy to these areas will further enhance your efforts. All of the chakra exercises are done primarily as outlined with the first level. I encourage you to record each exercise with your own voice. When you record them, be sure to have long pauses which give you time to implement the instructions during your actual meditation. Playback of these recordings during your relaxation period will affect your subconscious in an amazing and positive way. In addition, you will be able to focus more clearly on the exercise itself since you will not be attempting to recall the specific directions for that level.

The first center is located at the base of the spine and is associated with the color red, the tone of "C" and the sound of OOOOOO. This chakra represents the physical self and links us to the earth. Bones and skeletal structure connections are here. Thus, this center addresses security, courage and health. A metaphor is "standing up for one's self." The "flight or fight" mechanism connected with survival and creativity are governed here. This life preserving mechanism is controlled by our Adrenal Glands. Chronic struggle can cause the adrenal glands to be overstimulated. This is especially true when we struggle to dominate, are consistently depressed, "muddled" or feel caught in up-and-down-can't-figure-it-out situations.[1] Excessive epinephrine and norepinephrine are secreted. Unless the negative energy is resolved, acute and/or chronic disease is the ultimate result.

When you are feeling "spacey" or uncentered, try this. Sit calmly with your eyes closed. Quietly imagine a red ball turning at the base of your spine. If you have difficulty with the color think of a scarlet red fire engine until you have the color clearly in mind. Allow yourself to become totally engaged in seeing and feeling the sensations of color and energy at the base of your spine. Sometimes, forms, shapes, thoughts or other interferences may enter your mind. When this happens, effortlessly refocus your mind on the turning red ball. Let the energy and color flow through to the front of your body so that the entire body at that level appears to be a mass of red energy undulating or turning in on itself. After about five minutes, envision a cluster of energy gathering at the bottom of the red color. (It is okay to peek at a clock. Beginners sometimes imagine five minutes to be more like thirty.) Take another five or six minutes with this undulating energy. Now create an imaginary thread of red and drop an imaginary line from the red mass through the chair and floor into the earth. Imagine that this red thread somehow connects you to the earth. You may wish to let the thread spread like roots into the soil. Remain calm. Emphasize the weight of your body against the surface upon which you sit. Feel yourself getting heavier and heavier. Concentrate for a few minutes longer, feeling your weight as it connects to the red thread. Now, slowly count to five, feel the sensations in your entire body. Now, gradually open your eyes. When you first open your eyes focus on several points or articles in the room, one at a time, so that you "come back" bit-by-bit to the room. Note how "grounded" you feel. Experience the sensation of lucidity and solidarity. Take these feelings with you as you prepare to continue your day. There

---

[1]. The feelings cited here as associated with the various organs have been researched in ancient and modern literature and delineated by Dr. Scott Walker, founder of NeuroEmotional Technique.

is no limit to the number of occasions in which you may utilize this or any of the meditations. Your body, your progress and your degree of desire and enjoyment make that determination. Please note, however, that some people are so rested and energized by meditative relaxation that they become unable to sleep when they meditate in the late evening or at night.

The body's second center is located above the first center just beneath the navel. It is represented by the color orange, a "D" tone and the sound of ooooh. This center is concerned with connection to life and other people, vitality, change, sex, and relationships, including working with others. We are provided vivacity and vigor from the second energy center. Purpose, desire, pleasure and change are associated with this center. Obviously, there is reason to keep the energy of this center fluid, steady and vigorous.

When you feel a need for clear thinking, resolution or astute discernment in relationships, could use more stamina or have a desire to increase creativity, take time to sit silently and spin the orange ball. Let the color orange permeate and fill that area of the body between the navel and the base of the spine. The inside half of a big juicy orange or bright orange fire coals are nice to see as you begin this meditation. Amplify the color as you imagine a fiery spark of energy directly in its center. Gradually build the intensity of the spark. Let it grow in size and intensity to fill the area with the brightest possible orange light. As the color and light reach a crescendo, observe it. Now, feel the color spill into your body in waves much like the ocean does when it is building and lapping water against the shore. Notice the consolidation and rise of energy as it wells up through the color and then splashes through your body.

Use the vivid orange color to spotlight whatever you desire in a specific relationship. Outline a large frame within which you can produce a movie. Picture yourself relating to the other person in photographic detail as you outline precisely the manner in which you wish to function within that relationship. See yourself doing and being the person you desire to be. Make it as vivid and full of feeling as you can. Next, imagine a break in the frame at the bottom corner. Switch your full concentration back to the picture while at the same time you continue to see the vivid orange color. Let the frame become the color and the color become the frame. Use the orange color to fill any discordant feelings which remain in the picture. While still holding firmly to the scene in the picture, allow your mind to drain all dissidence, disharmonies and tension. Let it flow through the break in the orange frame. Be certain to let it all drain away. Now, emblazon your entire mind including the image, with the orange flame so that you burn out any remaining negativity. You may at this time ask any questions regarding this relationship. Let the answers and insights pour in. Focus on receiving the information with clarity. You may need to ask several times. Clarity will increase with practice. The Body/Mind always responds to positive questions with one or more solutions. Be persistent. When you feel complete, slowly count to five and gradually open your eyes. Acclimate to the room by focusing on objects and breathing deeply. Sit quietly for a few moments before continuing your day.

You may modify this meditation to include visualizations about your body size, shape or weight; your sensuality or sexual attractiveness; having a baby or becoming pregnant; sexual activity which is satisfying; sperm or egg production; giving and receiving love, affection, sexual advances or tangible items; emotions of tenderness, gentleness or self-confidence; creation of independence; to uncover and emancipate your creative urges; and anything else which is hindering you from standing firm in your own power and creativity.

The third center is located at the solar plexus, is yellow in color, has the tone of "E" and a sound of awwww. This area is in the center of the torso, in the pit of the stomach and seats the solar plexus. The energy of this area is related to "gut" feelings or emotions, self-realization, self-actualization, self-esteem, self-confidence and Will. It is the center of Personal Power. The associated organs are the stomach, pancreas and spleen. "Knots" in the stomach, feelings of nervousness, disgust, despair, lack of control, hopelessness, or being stifled may surface in the presence of blocked energy at this level.

This center is the area for focus during times of emotional upheaval or disappointment. Here is an exercise. As you calmly place your attention on the solar plexus, think of brilliant daffodils in full bloom. Let that magnificent yellow color build into a rich fullness which gorges the solar plexus. Allow the color to occlude all conscious thought so that in the moment nothing exists other than this spectacular, incandescent yellow. Sustain emphasis on the color as you begin to imagine it as whirling energy. Let the energy whirl in a manner which creates a vacuum through which all negative emotions may be spun into the atmosphere. Perhaps a yellow tornado sucks out the unwanted or negative emotion as it swirls past you. Maintain this concentration until the solar plexus center appears empty and translucent like the meat of a fresh lemon.

Next, create a spray of dusty rose color to mist over the area. Feel the calming effect being generated. Dusty rose is the color associated with self-love. We know that experiencing or sensing a loss of control in one's life usually is based on failure to value the self; to appreciate individuality, substance and self merits. The dusty rose color will magically and automatically fill some of that need when used with regularity and declaration of intent. Continue to saturate the solar plexus area with dusty rose light as you design a symbol that designates love to you. This symbol could be a rose, your father's hat, a beautiful bird or anything you desire. Let that rose-colored symbol appear at the top edge of the solar plexus and begin to multiply itself again and again until the entire lemon-yellow light in the solar plexus is filled with the rose-colored symbol.

Now, imagine a photograph of yourself being pushed into the symbols (images of love) and let the symbols push back through the photograph—fading back and forth, back and forth like water passing through a grate and back again, until you feel satisfied with the love you are embracing. Once more, let the energy spin in a manner that encircles the photograph and symbols. Slowly bring the spinning to a stop. Now, imagine the yellow ball of energy has returned. Let it pulse forward and backward through your body. Stop it. Spin it again until it is clear. Magnify the color and merge with it as you take it up, down and through your entire body. If it becomes muddy or more opaque, spin it clear again. Finally, blend the pure translucent yellow ball throughout your entire abdominal cavity, especially your stomach, spleen and pancreas. You may repeat this procedure as many times as you choose. When you feel ready, slowly count to five and gradually open your eyes. Acclimate to your environment. By clearing the personal power chakra and filling it with self-love and dignity, you may obtain perspective and lucidity.

The fourth energy center is located over the heart. The tone is "F sharp" and the sound is ahhhhh. Green is its color. As you may expect, it rules energies of love, healing, harmony, abundance, and Devine, unconditional love. The heart, lungs, immune and endocrine systems are governed here. Of course, you are aware that the heart is the source of life, itself. Without a heartbeat, we die. Without the pulse of blood throughout the body and its subsequent re-oxygenation and re-circulation, we die. It is a well established fact that blocked energy, especially emotional energy, will "break" the heart. That is, the heart will fail to function properly. Lack of emotion, feelings of desertion, and vulnerability reside in the heart energy.

Our lungs literally bring the breath of life. They are as vital as the heart in keeping us alive. Without the oxygen provided by the lungs, the heart can not function. The lungs also remove a tremendous amount of waste products from the body. Feelings of sadness, grief, dogma, defensiveness, yearning, and perfectionist behavior are associated with the lungs. And, endocrine system imbalance affects almost every bodily function. Imbalance in the endocrine system is reflected in feelings of paranoia, emotional instability, depletion, or non-emotive behavior. The entire fourth chakra clearly is the seat of love, forgiveness, compassion, understand and, in particular, love of self.

If you desire more harmony, abundance of life, healing or increased love, quiet yourself in your special space and spin a green ball over your heart. The color intensity and shade is that of a very clear emerald or summer grass. Green chlorophyll is Nature's healing/growth substance. Let the life-giving green become a beam of green light which vibrates more and more as it becomes brighter and brighter. After a few moments of spinning the vibrating color, allow the color to begin filling the heart itself. Totally fill the heart, then let a beam of green-colored light spill out to completely fill the chest cavity front to back, top to bottom and side to side. Now meld the light with the green ball and spin it again, this time as if superimposing the pulsing green light over the spinning ball. Simultaneously spread the color by creating a spray which fills your entire body.

You may choose to use the dusty rose color with the green, or imagine glistening emeralds attached to the ball giving off rainbows of all seven colors shooting out to various areas of your body. The heart center incorporates all love. Love is the major healing energy. Therefore, you may use this meditation to take healing green and loving energy to any other center or any part of the body. Be creative in your use of the color, light patterns and intensities. Take all the time you need. Venture out beyond the edges of your body. See how far away you can go while maintaining the same intensity of color. As the color expands out around you, imagine that you are in the center of a helium-filled balloon. The helium is very green and promotes peals of laughter as it surrounds you. Perhaps you will even laugh aloud. Envision small dusty rose hearts floating up from your heart and filling the green space inside the balloon. As the number of hearts grows, let spears of green light shine between and among them. Imagine that your heart and entire chest cavity opens wide to receive the healing light and love. Now, watch the light from your heart spin out to the world to give, receive and exchange love. Gently bring the green light back to your heart center. Make certain the light is crystal clear. Give the area some final attention before leaving the meditation. When finished, slowly count to five, gradually open your eyes and acclimate to your environment.

The fifth center is located in the throat and is associated with blue. Here the tone is G. The sound is Ehhhh. This center directs activity of communication and personal expression. It promotes truth and fosters appropriateness. Here, the energy is associated with the vocal cords, they thyroid gland and body metabolism which regulates the way we use body fuel. In addition, the hormones produced here affect brain function as well as respiratory and cardiovascular activities. Associated emotions are feelings of abandonment, being lost, and unrequited love.

To heighten, emphasize and promote truth, to beef up your integrity, increase clarity and develop your expressive abilities, spin a blue ball over your throat. Imagine the color of a clear afternoon sky. Vast, vacant, open blueness greets your eyes. Clouds are absent. You are seeing the blue hue that constitutes the throat center. Project the color into your throat area as you continue to sharpen your focus. Let the wonderful blue fill your entire neck and extend outward in front of you. Encourage the color to expand around your neck, across your shoulders and upward toward your jaw and the base of your head. Since throat centered energies feature communication and the vocal cords, voicing actual sounds during this meditation will assist in clearing and cleansing this center. If you are newcomer to deep relaxation exercises, it may be beneficial to first practice several sessions without sound so that you fully relax into the color. Hearing your own voice could take you out of relaxation unless you have learned to stay at that level.

Once the marvelous blue sky is cradling your throat and neck, observe a point at the base of the color about six inches out in front of you. Place a diamond in that spot and fill it with blue sky. Inspect the diamond carefully. Rainbows begin to form and float toward your throat. While the rainbows float, push the blue color out another six inches in front of your throat and visualize a second ball of blue. Rotate the ball into a whirl which goes faster and faster until there is a blurred sense of motion. The blurred motion changes into a hovering wisp of blue. Permit all negative thoughts and feelings to drift easily and quickly through the wisp, evaporating into the ethers. This is a time of letting go. When the space is empty, affirmations may effortlessly be placed into that space. You may concentrate on specific affirmations at the end of this (or any) meditation. When the affirmation is quite clear, refocus on the diamond. Let the clarity of the diamond equal the clarity of your affirmation(s) and vice versa. Imagine that the diamond clearly projects your affirmation(s) into your heart and mind as well as to the world around you. Here they are securely implanted.

# Puppet or Puppeteer / Dr. Nell Rodgers

Here is an additional step to perform during the first time you sit for this meditative relaxation. Transform the diamond into a blue topaz and let it swell to three times its size. The topaz begins to gently rise toward the center of your throat. Bring it about a foot out in front of you and see its brilliance begin to magnify and intensify. The brightness of the lighted topaz is almost startling. When you are satisfied with the magnitude and power of the gem, calmly move the topaz into the very center of your throat. Let it stay there so that you may call upon the topaz to clarify and cleanse your communication efforts at any time you wish. Of course this includes communication with yourself as well as for others. And, you may quickly access the topaz at any time or place simply by remembering.

When you have mastered the first part of this meditation, you are ready to add sound. Begin with saying Ehhhhhh. Establish a rhythm by emphasizing the sound while continuing to spin the ball. As the color is projected, embellish the sounds. Yield to the cadence and patterns as they swell from within you. Here, audibility and immersion of yourself into the color and sound are more important than volume. Energy, movement and intonation are the preferred result, especially in the beginning. When you are more comfortable, you will go into numerous progressions as you unfold. Once you have learned procedures for one area of energy development and opening, you will naturally and gracefully compose your own adventurous metamorphosis. Repeat the sounds at any volume and with variety until you feel a breakthrough or decide to quit. These are your meditations. The guidelines presented are a mere beginning. You will absolutely know when you have experienced a breakthrough. If you are tired or the process feels too stressful, quit. Return to the sounds in a later meditation.

When working with the throat center, a variation for enhancing your change includes the use of words. If you feel too inhibited to say the thing which longs to be said, or fear exploding into heavy, forceful, graphic or passionate sounds, continue with the sound of Ehhhhh until you feel comfortable enough to speak. You will have many opportunities as you set a routine pattern for your relaxation sessions. Once you have begun to talk, the words will probably flow easily. Harboring dissension and discordant thoughts and images is detrimental, so let them be released. Although this part of the procedure is optional at any time, it is useful to end the meditation with the bright topaz in the throat as a symbol of light and clarity. The use of words, like the sounds, may be interjected at the time you are letting thoughts drift through the wisp of blue. One option is to imagine yourself saying all the things you wish to say and to whom you wish to say them, including yourself. Be explicit and hold nothing back. This is another of those moments when the more you let go and totally empty yourself, the better you will feel and the more energized you will become. No one will ever know these thoughts unless you later choose to tell them. As the words and images emerge, experience them, then let them be sucked out into and through the blue wisp of color. They will fall into a void and become nothing. Giving audible voice to the words is unnecessary but okay. You will discover that seeing and feeling the words disappear into the void may be more powerful and freeing than giving voice to them. Try both and then decide. Perhaps you will choose to alternate using audible voice with imagined words and images. Continue this activity until you feel emptied. Emotional releases such as tears, laughter, groans, or body movement may occur. Let it happen. You are clearing the way for new programming and establishing freedom.

Spin the blue ball a final time, drawing out all energy or different colors. Make certain that the entire neck is a crystal clear transparent sky blue. Now let the truth about the situation you are clearing melt through the vibration of color. Own your responsibility in the circumstance and let it go. Complete the meditation as you have with others. Leave the topaz in the center of your throat. Count to five, slowly open your eyes and acclimate to the room.

The sixth center is located between and just above the eyebrows. The color is indigo and is depicted by a stark, clear, very dark grayish-blue midnight sky. The tone and sounds are A and Ihhhhhh. Inner vision, intuition, wisdom, alchemy and idealism are centered here. The Pituitary gland, the eyes, ears, nose and parts of the nervous system are the focus at this energy center. Hormonal activity is mediated by the pituitary gland and is actually an extension of one part of the brain. The eyes, ears and nose are involved in numerous emotions and functions, from weeping and lubrication, to equilibrium, filtration of air and the "smell of danger."

For this meditation, pinpoint the area between and just above the eyebrows. As you spin an indigo ball, imagine a crescendo of color culminating in waves which radiate out like circles of light from the center to the outer circumference of the ball. Some people like to visualize the light as rays similar to those of a radio tower. Picture the base of the brain at about two inches to the inside of the mid-brow point. The pituitary gland sits here. Imagine this as the center of your nervous system. Connect this center with the core of the indigo ball. Fire off the light circles and send a shaft of the colored light directly out in front of you. Imagine that the Universe is adding to the intensity of the shaft of light. See it intensify in color and size. Keeping the shaft of indigo light intact, draw energy through it and into the pituitary gland. Let the light spread until it permeates the entire brain. Now, return to the mid-brow point. There are two emotional points located on the forehead; one above the center of each eyebrow. Make connecting beacons of light extending outward from the mid-brow point to each emotional point. Let these beacons begin to pulsate. Allow the pulse to get stronger, larger and more intense moment by moment until each bursts open with energy. Watch your old emotional garbage spew forth and drain out. Gather it all into a single bundle. Imagine that you energetically fling that bundle of negative emotions to the sun where it will be depolarized and turned into positive energy. Continue this process until the emotional points are completely empty of negativity and discordant emotions. When you are ready, fill the emotional points with streams of indigo light. Make the points three-dimensional and let the light swell to about three times their size. Intensify the light even more if you can. You may choose to stop here, depending upon the amount of time and the degree of intensity in the meditation thus far. If this is your choice, refocus on your body, slowly open you eyes and acclimate to the room.

Organs or parts of the body may serve as a focal point for insight into how you dramatize life. The following are optional, modified versions that may be added to this meditation. Each option may also become a separate meditation. Any or all may be combined in any manner. That is your choice as you continue your meditative relaxation experiences. You may choose any organ or part of your body. As an example, in this illustration I will use difficulty with the liver. The liver is located on the right side of the body beneath the lower ribs. For this exercise, you will take yourself to the state where the indigo light has refilled the emptied emotional points. While the light bulges, focus that light energy so that it merges into a single beam out in front of your forehead. Send this radiating beam in an arch of indigo light that ends in the liver. Fill the liver with the light. Do not be concerned about the size and exact location of the organs. The body intuitively knows your intent and will accept your direction perfectly. When the liver (or other organ) is filled with indigo light, sit quietly with that feeling for a few moments. Turn the beam of light into a tunnel. The inside of the tunnel is clear and the walls are very heavy, robust indigo light. Become totally engaged in this activity. Let yourself go. Gently ask the liver to release any negative emotions being harbored there. Allow old emotional traumas to easily surface and watch them float up the tunnel toward the emotional points. Just before they reach the emotional points, open a side gate to the tunnel and watch them float toward and into the sun. Take your time. You may repeat the question to the liver in order to release everything to the tunnel.

After the tunnel is clear, forgive yourself for your part in holding on to or creating the negativity. If someone is related to the negative emotion or incident, forgive the transgressor----including yourself---and send that person a beam of light through the tunnel gate. Give thanks for increased freedom and healing as you permit the tunnels of light to subtly disappear. Refocus on the mid-brow point. Spin the indigo ball until you feel clear. You may stop here or continue.

Indigo light is still the focus. Reach into your brain/mind and pull up one of your dreams, something you have long wanted to be or do. (Your agenda may be set prior to sitting for this meditation.) Make a large bubble of light about a foot out in front of you. Place your dream inside the bubble. Sit with this picture until you have meticulously filled in every detail of how you want the situation to be. What are you doing? How are you doing it? Imagine the clothing you are wearing, your precise facial expressions, how you feel, your exact posture, gait, your hair style, the tone, volume and timbre of your voice, the words you are using, what you are saying, who, if anyone, is present or any other details you wish to include. Experience your dream precisely as you want it to be when it is achieved. When the picture is as you desire it to be and you are feeling the excitement and joy of your dream, bring all the feelings of that picture into your physical body at the same time you are concentrating on the details of the picture. When you have exquisite details and robust feelings, you are you ready to fill the bubble with light to the point of bursting it open. As the bubble bursts, both the picture and you are catapulted to a bright light beyond the horizon. After a few moments of being there, gradually and gently float back "into yourself." Redirect your attention to the mid-brow. Spin the indigo color ball faster and faster taking it away from you. Bring it close in; then out again and back. Continue to spin the ball until it is as clear as a piece of indigo blown glass. Let it melt into nothingness. When you are ready, count to five, gradually open your eyes and acclimate to the room.

This experience will activate and balance the nervous system as well as titillate your imagination and tease out your genuine desires. New information often sifts through during meditation at the sixth level. Emotional equilibrium can result. The nervous system is the hub of all activity.

## A Companion Guidebook

The seventh center is located at the crown of the head. Its color is that of wild violets, with a tone of B and the sound of EEEEEEE. The crown chakra governs purpose and represents final integration and transmutation of energy that may be out of alignment with the Higher Power. Spiritual Will, inspiration, Divine wisdom, selfless service, unity and understanding reside here. Blocked energy at this level will result in feelings of being disconnected, wanting more, or persistent struggle. There may be a lack of life-direction or life-purpose. The brain and Central Nervous System are associated with this center. Of course, the Central Nervous System, which includes the brain, governs, regulates and commands the body in all its functions. Everything from sexual excitement and heart rhythms to bone growth, digestion, pregnancy and urine is directed by the Central Nervous System. Negative feelings include depression and confusion.

If you yearn for a closeness with your God-force, clear this center. The example given here focuses on purpose but you may use any topic or integration of energy. For this exercise, write down your purpose as you now perceive it. Even if it feels ridiculous and uncomfortable, write something. Meditating will help "self-correct" anything which may be off course. Read your statement several times. Close your eyes and concentrate on the crown of your head. Bring in a violet light and spin the energy ball above and around the crown of your head. Brighten and amplify the color, always accentuating the most vivid color possible. When you think it is bright enough, push a bit further to amplify it even more. This is your connecting link to the universe. (Do not confuse this with or substitute it for your customary avenues and links to your Higher Power. You will probably still want to use those connections as you normally do. Your spiritual/religious beliefs are different from the work with meditative relaxation exercises.)

After a few moments of spinning the ball of light, allow the color to transmute into a stark, white light. Keep spinning and turning the white light while drawing up a part of it to the space above your head, creating a spotlight effect on you. Move the spotlight out in front of you if it will help you to see the picture more clearly. Place an image of yourself in the center of the spotlight. Mentally take a position of surrender, whatever that means to you. For some it will be kneeling, for others it may be lying prone, sitting, your palms extended upward or some other position. Mentally state your purpose as written. Silently surrender to that purpose. Become willing to do whatever is necessary to fulfill your purpose. Affirm that the fulfillment of purpose is in the best interest of you and all people concerned. Notice what you feel as you are consumed with the act of surrender. Mentally state phrases such as "I surrender to my purpose." "I'm on purpose." "I divinely fulfill my purpose." "My purpose is Divine" and so forth. Formulate those phrases which are best suited to you and repeat them again and again. Let them become automatic in your thinking. If you have difficulty with the statements, such as stumbling on the words or being unable to say them exactly the same way each time, simply continue to repeat them until you are comfortable and there is no resistance.

Now move the words as a group to the right side of your brain. Hold the words there as you bring the white light down into your head. Expand the light to fill your entire head. Concentrate on projecting the words being held in the right brain upward through the light. Push each word individually up through the light. Hold them together, then let the words drop downward. Project them upward collectively. Let them drop. Lift them individually again. Let then drop; now collectively. Do this rotation for two or three minutes, ending with the words high inside you head.

## Puppet or Puppeteer / Dr. Nell Rodgers

Merge violet light with the white until the entire head is filled with violet. Bring the violet light through the crown of your head and recreate the violet whirling ball. Spin it clockwise. Hold that spin while creating a superimposing white light turning counterclockwise. Focus and concentration will be necessary for this action. After a few moments, return to the violet clockwise spinning light. Now slowly switch to a white light which is received into the crown of your head from high above you. Consolidate all your energy into receiving the white light, moving it downward, filling every cell of your entire body. Stay with this feeling as long as you desire. When you feel complete, merge the white light with the violet light. Now, let the violet light spin very slowly as it dissipates into a mist of light and ultimately disappears. Count to five, gradually open your eyes and acclimate to your environment.

Balancing your energy fields can be valuable for changing many things at once, letting go of unwanted emotions and unfavorable thoughts, or for programming particular, specific shifts in your thoughts or behavior. Clarity in any energy field, regardless of that center's active focus, can affect a specific activity. It may also influence several aspects of behavior and responses at the same time. For instance a back problem, frustration with a friend or co-worker and having to engage in unwanted activity at home, may all be interconnected. By shifting the energy of any aspect of the body's centers, all of these areas will be affected; some more than others, obviously.

Perhaps you have experienced something similar to the following example. Sidney was angry at his wife and they argued. Later in the day, he had a tightness and pain in his shoulder. They were scheduled to attend a birthday dinner for a friend whom they honored. When Sidney got involved conversationally with his pals, the pain left. Laughter and camaraderie shifted his energy. On the other hand, Sidney's wife had a headache later in the day. She did a meditative relaxation before going to the party and arrived there pain-free. In truth, it does not matter if the energy is shifted consciously or subconsciously. However, through conscious efforts, new pathways for positive affirmation of self can result. Clarity of thought and intention as well as the elimination of unwanted behaviors can be developed. Time, patience and persistence can bring genuine internal guidance.

Energy balancing exercises as presented here are only examples. There are innumerable ways and an array of methods that may be used to enhance your life through alpha relaxation. If meditation is especially effective for you, I suggest that you find a mentor or coach to assist you in going further than these exercises may take you. Countless books are also available on the subject. Most of them give explicit directions so that you can experience what you are learning about a particular method. Check with a bookstore, a friend or the appendix in the back of this guidebook. Experiment and create your own methods. If you decide to read these exercises aloud into a tape recorder microphone, you may discover after a few experiences that you can modify them yourself. Of course, use the recordings privately so that you have the freedom you desire for experimenting. Remember that the sound of directives presented in your own voice have even greater clout in the subconscious. Explore and practice. Find the perfect balancing program for yourself and practice it often.

# Appendix:

# Resources, Information and Practitioners

*It is not because things are difficult that we do not dare; it is because we do not dare that they are difficult.*

Seneca
(5 BC - 65)

*The ultimate measure of a man is not where he stands in moments of comfort and convenience, but where he stands at times of challenge and controversy.*

Martin Luther King, Jr.
*Strength to Love*
1963

# A Companion Guidebook

## Resources for Practitioners Who Assist With Belief Changes

**The O.N.E. Foundation**
(NeuroEmotional Technique™)
199 Village Park Way, Suite 201A
Encinitas, CA 92024
(800) 638-1411
E-mail: office@onefoundation.org
Website: NetMindBody.com
Safe, gentle and effective release of NeuroEmotional Complexes which keep us stuck in unwanted patterns.

**PSYCH-K™ Center**
P O Box 548
Crestone, CO 81131
(719) 256-4995
Website: www.psych-k.com
Safe, effective, user-friendly way to rewrite the software of your mind to change the print-out of your life.

**EMDR Institute, Inc.**
P O Box 750
Watsonville, CA 95077
Website: www.emds.com
E-mail: inst@emdr.com
(831) 761-1040
Fax: (831) 761-1204
Eye Movement Desensitization and Reprocessing is a safe, user friendly information processing therapy.

**NLP University**
P O Box 1112
Ben Lomond, CA 95005
(831) 336-3457
Fax: (831) 336-5854
E-mail: teresanlp@aol.com
Links from NLP Co-Founder John Grinder to NLP workshops, training and consultation.

117

**Pure NLP™**
P O Box 424
Hopstrong, NJ 07843
(973) 770-3600
Links from NLP Co-Founder Richard Bandler to NLP Institutes, Health & Fitness, and Solutions.

**Core Belief Engineering**
Elly Roselle
Core Belief Engineering Ltd.
15459 Semiahmoo Avenue
White Rock, BC. V4B 1T7
Phone: (604) 536-7402 or 1(888) 771-3707
Fax: (604) 536-0804
Email: ERoselle-CBE@email.msn.com
Website: http://www.corebelief.net
Allows conscious re-engineering of outdated beliefs and decisions, and replacement with more open and inclusive expressions of self.

**Holographic Repatterning™ Association**
P O Box 14
Aragon, NM 87820
(505) 533-6060
Fax: (240) 363-6117
hra@holographic.org
www.holographic.org
A process that makes possible the creation of positive change in any limiting area of life.

# Information and Professional Resources in Art, Dance, Humor, Music

**American Art Therapy Association, Inc.**
1202 Allanson Road
Mundelein, IL 60060
(847) 949-6064
Fax: (847) 566-4580
E-mail: info@arttherapy.org
Website: www.arttherapy.org
Dedicated to the belief that the creative process involved in the making of art is healing and life-enhancing.

**American Association for Music Therapy**
  8455 Colesville Road
  Suite 1000
  Silver Springs, MD 20910
  (301) 589-3300
  Fax: (301) 589-5175
  E-mail: info@musictherapy.org
  Website: www.musictherapy.org
  Learn benefits of music therapy and increase access to quality music therapy services

**American Association for Therapeutic Humor**
  1951 W Camelback Rd
  Suite 445
  Phoenix, AZ 85015
  (602) 995-1454
  Fax: (602) 995-1449
  E-mail: office@aath.org
  Website: www.aath.org
  Learn values and therapeutic uses of humor and laughter.

**American Dance Therapy Association**
  10632 Little Pateuxent Parkway
  2000 Century Plaza, Suite 108
  Columbia, MD 21044
  (410) 997-4040
  Fax: (410) 997-4048
  E-mail: info@adta.org
  Website: www.adta.org
  Resource for professional education and competent professionals in the field of dance/movement therapy.

**National Association for Music Therapy**
  10632 Little Pateuxent Parkway
  Columbia, MD 21044
  (410) 997-4040
  Fax: (410) 997-4048
  E-mail: info@adta.org
  Website: www.adta.org
  Resource for standards of competence for professional music therapists.

## Resources for Body-Mind Relationships Information

**Association for Humanistic Psychology**
1516 Oak Street, # 320A
Alameda, CA 94501
E-mail: asoffice@aol.com
Website: www.ahpweb.org
Nurtures people's ability to use their conscious mind to change, grow and actively create their lives.

**Center for Mindfulness in Medicine, Healthcare and Society**
University of Massachusetts Medical Center
Stress Reduction Clinic
55 Lake Avenue North
Worcester, MA 01655
(508) 856-2656
Fax: (508) 856-1977
E-mail: mindfulness@umassmed.edu
Website: www.umassmed.edu/cfm
Promoting the practice and integration of mindfulness in the lives of individuals, institutions and society.

**Institute Of Noetic Sciences**
101 San Antonio Rd
Petaluma, CA 94952
(707) 775-3500
Fax: (707) 781-7420
E-mail: membership@noetic.org
Website: www.noetic.org
Non-profit organization conducts and sponsors research into the potential and powers of consciousness, including perceptions, beliefs, attention and intuition.

**Mind-Body Health Sciences, Inc.**
393 Dixon Road
Boulder, CO 80401
(303) 440-8460
Fax: (303) 440-7580
E-mail: luziemas@aol.com
Resource Information

## Resources for Therapies and Professionals Which Engage Body and Mind

**American Society for the New Identity Process**
131 Colonial Hill Drive
Wallingford, CT 06518
(888) 912-1891

**Body of Knowledge/Hellerwork**
406 Berry Street
Mt. Shasta, CA 96067
(916) 926-2500

**East-West Academy of Healing Arts**
117 Topaz Way
San Francisco, CA 94131
(415) 647-5745
E-mail info@eastwestqi.com
Website: www.eastwestqi.citysearch.com

**Emotional Freedom Technique (EFT)**
P O Box1393
Gualala CA 95445
(707) 705-2848
Website: www.emofree.com

**NeuroLink**
P O Box 74176
Market Road
Auckland, New Zealand
USA (866) 263-0869
E-mail: neurolink@attglobal.net
Website: www.neurolinkglobal.com

**Qigong Institute**
561 Berkeley Ave
Menlo Park, CA 94025
Website: www.qigonginstitute.org

PUPPET OR PUPPETEER / DR. NELL RODGERS

**Rubenfeld Center**
115 Waverly Place
New York, NY 10011
(212) 254-5100
Fax: (212) 254-1174
E-mail: rubenfeld@aol.com

**School for Body-Mind Centering**
189 Pond View Drive
Amherst, MA 01002
(413) 256-8615
(413) 256-8239
info@bodymindcentering.com
Website: www.bodymindcentering.com

**Total Body Modification (TBM)**
1904 Foxmore Circle
Sandy, UT 84092
(801) 571-2411
Fax: (801) 576-0806

**United States Association for Body Psychotherapy**
7831 Woodmont Ave
Suite 294
Bethesda, MD 20814
(202) 466-1619
Fax: (281) 370-0280
E-mail: usabp@usabp.org
Website: www.usabp.org

# RESOURCES FOR VISUALIZATION, GUIDED IMAGERY AND HYPNOTHERAPY

**Academy for Guided Imagery**
PO Box 2070
Mill Valley, CA 94942
(800) 726-2070
Fax: (415) 389-9342
Website: www.interactiveimagery.com

## A Companion Guidebook

**American Imagery Institute**
4016 Third Avenue
San Diego, CA 92103
(619) 298-7502
Fax: (619) 633-3393

**American Association of Professional Hypnotherapists**
4149 El Comino Way
Palo Alto, CA 94306
(650) 323-3224
Website: www.aap.org

**American Society of Clinical Hypnosis**
140 Bloomingdale Rd
Bloomingdale, IL 60108
(630) 980-4740
Fax: (630) 351-8490
E-mail: info@asch.net
Website: www.asch.net

**Chopra Center for Well-Being**
2013 Costa del Mar Rd
Carlsbad, CA 92009
(888) 424-6772
Fax: (760) 931-7572
E-mail: info@chopra.com
Website: www.chopra.com

**Himalayan International Institute of Yoga, Science and Philosophy**
RR 1, Box 400
Honesdale, PA 18431
(800) 822-4547
(717) 253-5551
Fax: (717) 253-9078
E-mail: info@himalayaninstute.org
Website: www.himalayaninstitute.org

**Institute of Transpersonal Psychology**
744 San Antonio Rd
Palo Alto, CA 94303
(650) 493-4430
Fax: (650) 493-6835
Website: www.itp.edu

**Milton Erickson Foundation**
    3606 North 24th Street
    Phoenix, AZ 85016
    (602) 956-6196
    Website: www.erickson-foundation.org

# Resources for Nutrition Information

**American College of Nutrition**
    300 S Duncan Ave
    Suite 225
    Clearwater, FL 33755
    (727) 446-6086
    Fax: (727) 446-6202
    E-mail: office@am-coll-nutr.org
    Website: www.am-coll.nutr.org

**George Ohsawa Macrobiotic Foundation**
    P O box 3998
    Chico, CA 95927
    (800) 232-2373
    (530) 566-9765
    E-mail: gomf@earthlink.net
    Website: www.gomf.macrobiotic.org

# Resources for Holistic, Traditional, Alternative and Complementary Health Care

**American Chiropractic Association**
    1701 Clarendon Boulevard
    Arlington, VA 22209
    (800) 956-4636
    Fax: (703) 243-2593
    E-mail: memberinfo@amerchiro.org
    Website: www.amerchiro.org

**American Holistic Medical Association**
  12101 Menaul Blvd. NE, Suite C
  Albuquerque, NM 97112
  (505) 292-7788
  Fax: (505) 793-7582
  E-mail: info@holisticmedicine.org
  Website: www.holisticmedicine.org

**American Holistic Nurses Association**
  P O Box 2130
  Flagstaff, AZ 86003
  (800) 278-2462
  E-mail: info@ahna.org
  Website: www.ahna.org

**American Polarity Therapy Association**
  P O Box 19858
  Boulder, CO 80308
  (303) 545-2080
  Fax: (303) 545-2161
  E-mail: HQ@polaritytherapy.org
  Website: www.polaritytherapy.org

**Association for Applied Psychophysiology and Biofeedback**
  10200 West 44th Avenue, Suite 304
  Wheat Ridge, CO 80033
  (303) 422-8892
  Fax: (303) 422-8436
  E-mail: aapb@resourcenter.com
  Website: www.aapb.org

**Association for Network Chiropractic**
  444 West Main Street
  Longmont, CA 80501
  (303) 678-8101

**Biofeedback Certification Institute of America**
  10200 West 44th Avenue, Suite 30
  Wheat Ridge, CO 80033
  (303) 420-2902
  Fax (303) 422-8894
  E-mail: bcia@resourcenter.com
  Website: www.bcia.org

**Bowen Research and Training Institute**
   38541 U S Highway 19 North
   Palm Harbor, FL 34684
   (727) 937-9077
   Fax: (727) 942-9687
   E-mail: bowenresearch@earthlink.net
   Website: www.bowen.org

**Feldenkrais Guild**
   3611 SW Hood Ave, Suite 100
   Portland, OR 97239
   (800) 775-2118
   (503) 221-6612
   Fax: (503) 221- 6616
   Website: www.feldenkrais.com

**Foot Reflexology Awareness Association**
   P O Box 7622
   Mission Hills, CA
   (818) 361-0528
   Website: www.fraa.net

**Foundation for Shamanic Studies**
   P O Box 1939
   Mill Valley, CA 94942
   (415) 380-8282
   E-mail: info@shamanicstudies.com
   Website: www.shamanism.org

**Institute of Core Energetics**
   115 East 23rd Street
   New York, NY 10010
   (212) 982-9637
   Website: www.coreenergeticseast.org

**International College of Applied Kinesiology**
   6405 Metcalf Ave
   Shawnee Mission, KS 66202
   (913) 384-5336
   E-mail: icak@usa.net
   Website: www.icak.com

**International Rolf Institute**
205 Canyon Blvd
Boulder, CO 80306
(303) 449-5903
(800) 530-8875
Fax: (303) 449-5978

**Neurostructural Technique (NST)**
Optimal Wellness Center
1443 W Schaumburg, IL 60194
E-mail: webmaster@mercola.com
Website: www.mercola.com

**North American Society of Teachers of Alexander Technique**
P O Box 60008
Florence, MA 01062
(800) 473-0620
Fax: (413) 584-3097
Website: www.alexander.com

**Reiki Alliance**
204 N Chestnut St
Kellogg, ID 838377
Fax: (208) 7834848
E-mail: info@reikialliance.com
Website: www.reikialliance.com

**Touch for Health Kinesiology Association**
P O Box 392
New Castle, OH 45344
(800) 466-8342
Fax: (937) 845-3909
E-mail: admin@tfhka.org
Website: www.tfhka.org

**Trager Institute**
24800 Chogrin Blvd, Suite 205
Beachwood, OH 44122
(216) 896-9383
E-mail: trager@trager.com
Website: www.trager.com

## Other Resources

**American Preventive Medical Association**
    9912 Georgetown Pike, Suite D-2
    P O Box 458
    Great Falls, VA 22066
    (800) 230-2762
    Fax: (703) 759-6711
    E-mail: info@healthfreedom.net
    Website: www.healthfreedom.net

**American Academy of Anti-Aging Medicine**
    1510 Montana St
    Chicago, IL 60614
    (773) 528-8500
    E-mail: info@worldhealth.com
    Website: www.worldhealth.com

# About the Author

The author has spent most of her life learning about how humans function; what makes us behave and respond. At an early age she decided to become immersed in learning how to help herself and others tap into their own resources to more fully greet and express life. She has continued this exploration because she deeply believes in the resilience and power of the human spirit and our inherent wisdom. When a door closed, she simply opened another and another until she gained the understanding, information or insight she sought. Because of her tenacious persistence and commitment she has acquired a breadth of experience and knowledge far beyond that of the average professional.

Dr. Nell, as her clients like to call her, has served as a registered nurse, a psychotherapist, associate university faculty and as a doctor of chiropractic in her private holistic health practice. Her presence, skills, compassion and knowledge have made her a sought-after lecturer, mentor, clinician and consultant. The demand for her coaching and consultation skills have taken her throughout the United States and foreign countries. Those who work with her repeatedly speak of her kindness, sensitivity and giving spirit as she implements her down-to-earth practical programs of care and learning. Her willingness to do whatever is needed is prominent in her philosophy of life. Her suggestions and prescriptions for healing your body or your life are based in experience and a broad education combined with gentleness, honor and respect for others.

Early in her career, Dr. Nell was presented the "Outstanding Nurse" medal, an award created by the hospital medical staff as a means of honoring her contributions. She never looked back and has continued in service to others for more than 50 years, receiving numerous tributes and acknowledgments. Her peers, her clients and her students admire her genuineness and recognize her wit and wisdom which is grounded in a deep faith in the human potential. She actively practices what she preaches and firmly believes that we are charged with the responsibility of fulfilling our potential, be it trash collector, multimillionaire or artist. In that regard, she has an uncanny ability to see the Essence of those she encounters and consistently takes the time to encourage individuals to believe in themselves.

Throughout her life, Dr. Nell has searched for inner clarity and life's substance. At age 40, in order to scrutinize her purpose and connect with her deepest self, she left a prestigious career, sold her home along with most of her possessions and spent 14 months traveling, hiking, exploring and backpacking into wilderness areas. The adventures and intensity of her experiences, the people she met, the chosen isolation, her introspection and deep connection with her own spirit in the presence of nature dramatically altered her life. As she encountered, overcame, pushed through, meditated, stretched physical limits and basked in the sheer beauty of nature she was molded into a wiser and more authentic woman who exemplifies her expanded sense of self as she relates to the world and its inhabitants.

In *Puppet or Puppeteer*, the author combines her teaching skills, her knowledge and personal experiences to convey to the reader practical information which can be used to broaden personal resources and uncover limiting beliefs. Her ability to guide the reader through life-changing experiences becomes obvious.

# Quick Order Form

Fax Orders: 1-404-371-8833
Mail Postal Orders to:
**Awesome Press**
**P. O. Box 1071**
**Decatur, GA 30031-1071**

**Please send the following books.** I understand that within 30 days I may return any of them for a full refund, for any reason, no questions asked.

| Quantity | Title | SubTotal |
|---|---|---|
| | *Puppet or Puppeteer: Choose the Life You Want to Live* - $24.95 | |
| | *Puppet or Puppeteer: Choose the Life You Want to Live - A Companion Guidebook* - $19.95 | |
| | Georgia Residents, please add 7% sales **tax** | |
| | **Shipping:** $4.00 for first book and $3.00 for each additional book. International Airmail: $9.00 for first book and $5.00 for each additional book | |
| | **Total:** | |

Name: _____

Address: _____

City, State, Zip: _____

Phone: _____ Email: _____

Method of Payment: (circle one) Check / MC / V / DIS

Card No.: _____ Exp. Date: _____

Name on Card: _____

Signature: _____

Visit our web site at: www.AwesomePress.com

www.ingramcontent.com/pod-product-compliance
Lightning Source LLC
Chambersburg PA
CBHW080514110426
42742CB00017B/3115